Girl,
Uncoded

Girl, Uncoded

A Memoir of Passion, Betrayal, and Eventual Blessings

Brandi Dredge

SHE WRITES PRESS

Published 2024
Printed in the United States of America
Print ISBN: 978-1-64742-808-2
E-ISBN: 978-1-64742-809-9
Library of Congress Control Number: 2024909057

For information, address:
She Writes Press
1569 Solano Ave #546
Berkeley, CA 94707

Interior Design by Andrea Reider

She Writes Press is a division of SparkPoint Studio, LLC.

Names and identifying characteristics have been changed to protect the privacy of certain individuals.

A NOTE FROM THE AUTHOR

What I love about memoirs is how memories are mined to unearth the feelings associated with real-life events; then, by using creative techniques, they are shaped into stories that immerse you in worlds built on truths. Before you enter mine, I would like to welcome you and let you know that I am so glad you are here.

I also want you to know that this memoir is a work of creative nonfiction that reflects my present recollections of experiences over time. While this memoir is a true account of events in my life, all names have been changed, some events have been compressed, some dialogue has been recreated, and some locations, dates, and characteristics have been changed.

As a memoirist I have set out to tell you the truth; however, I recognize that truth is only mine. The views expressed in the story are solely mine, and while I have a right to share them, I wish to cause no harm to those who appear in my work.

The path of healing is messy but beautiful, and though I have chosen to change the names of others to protect identities, I have chosen to change mine in the story to honor my path by using this creative expression to reflect letting go and the power of transformation.

Although changes were made, this story is, to the best of my memory, an accurate portrayal of a complicated story that deals with sexual offenses and abuse. I have taken great lengths to ensure the subject matter is dealt with in a compassionate and respectful manner; however, it may be troubling for some readers. Discretion is advised.

To the survivors,
the ones who had to learn to carry tough things.

TABLE OF CONTENTS

Prologue: The Beginning of the End xi

Chapter 1: A Girl Who Met a Man 1

Chapter 2: Labeled: Young, Dumb, Pregnant 11

Chapter 3: Plans, Pleas, and Diarrhea 22

Chapter 4: My Wedding Day, His Ploy 30

Chapter 5: Stay 38

Chapter 6: Unprotected 52

Chapter 7: How Did I Get Here, Again? 66

Chapter 8: Driveway 87

Chapter 9: Intuition 96

Chapter 10: Exit Plan 103

Chapter 11: Needed 112

Chapter 12: This Little Clown 124

Chapter 13: Behind the Glass 136

Chapter 14: Memory 149

Chapter 15: Evidence 160

Chapter 16: Daddy's Hands 169

Chapter 17: The Frame 179

Chapter 18: Infected 190

Chapter 19: The Rules 204

Chapter 20: More Likely 213

Chapter 21: Suffocate or Survive 228

Chapter 22: Who I Am 239

Chapter 23: The Evidence of Blessings 257

Epilogue 266

Acknowledgments 269

About the Author 271

THE BEGINNING
OF THE END

When you tell your story, you must start from the beginning. I heard those very words—*start from the beginning*—one cold December morning as I sat across from a sergeant with the sheriff's office and prepared to give my statement. His fingers lined up on the keyboard, ready to type my every word, his eyes glaring so intensely at me that I just knew he saw the big, pulsating lump inside my throat. The beat of my heart grew faster as panic took its place within my chest, and I silently told myself *breathe, Caroline, just breathe.* To avoid eye contact, I fixed my gaze on the white papers stretched across the desk.

"Start from the beginning," he said again and then added, "When did you meet your husband?"

The question was simple; the words should have flowed. I knew the answer, yet all I could think was *How did I get here?*

That question was not a beginning question. It usually came at an ending, when a choice I made led to an outcome very different from what I had hoped for. I asked this question when I wanted to get clarity or validation for what I did or didn't do, what I said or didn't say. The answer was elusive, like a child playing hide-and-seek, but I looked high and low, trying to tag the truth that was always hidden from me.

How is this my life? How did I not see this coming? How did I get here? I was a wife sitting between the cold gray concrete walls of the sheriff's department, giving a statement regarding evidence related to a crime my husband had committed. Then, ready or not . . . I found the answer, and it became my beginning.

CHAPTER 1

A GIRL WHO
MET A MAN

"Did you know the guy who lives at this apartment is a stripper?" asked my friend.

"What? Is he?" I said. I was intrigued. At sixteen, I'd never met—or even seen—a stripper before. "I can't wait to see him!"

We were sitting on a couch with several boys from our high school. The boys had rebelled against their parents and moved in with their manager at the fast-food restaurant where they all worked, who was, apparently, also a stripper. Though I didn't know these boys well, I had been at a party at this apartment after a basketball game just a week earlier. I knew it was the go-to place for high school students who were looking to have unsupervised fun.

There were plenty of rumors about this apartment— girls in my class whispered how cute the man who owned the apartment was, while the boys talked about how this twenty-four-year-old man would buy alcohol for them and their friends. With every word that buzzed around the halls, my interest grew. Thoughts of meeting him swirled within my sixteen-year-old mind long before I heard the stripper rumor. It only added to my growing fascination.

As I sat there making small talk, I secretly hoped tonight would be the night I would finally get to see him. I didn't have long to wait. The front door creaked open, footsteps pushed across the floor of the front hallway, and within moments there stood the mystery man himself.

He had golden-tanned skin and eyes as deep blue as the sea. He was tall, muscular, and wore his coal-black hair down to his jaw. I shyly glanced at him, feeling the pink tinge filling my cheeks. As giggles started to rise within, I looked away and leaned my shoulder into my friend. She and I quietly exchanged chuckles and glances as he talked briefly with his roommates before walking out of the room and down the hallway to the bathroom.

I knew where he went thanks to a large rectangular mirror hanging on the wall opposite the bathroom; in its reflection I was able to see him lathering his face with white shaving cream. Pushing my shyness aside, I thought about how much more fun this night would be if I interacted with him instead of spectating from the couch. I headed to the bathroom.

"I want to shave your face!" I declared, trying to sound grown-up and alluring. I had plenty of experience flirting with guys my age, but the prospect of flirting with this "worldly" *man* was exhilarating.

He looked at me with his eyebrows raised. "Have you ever shaved a man's face before?"

"No," I playfully replied. "Will you let me try?" I admitted that he would undoubtedly receive a few nicks but that the experience would be worth the pain.

He smiled. "Okay." He said his name was Gary Richard Downey.

Gary Richard and I began a game of cat and mouse, in which he thrust the handle out to me and then pulled it back every time I reached for it. We both laughed, and he finally placed the razor in my hand. He sat down on the toilet seat, and I squatted in front of him and gently placed the razor on his cheek.

As I lowered the blade, he jerked and grabbed his neck. "You cut me!" he said, but I could tell his voice was teasing.

"Stop! No, I didn't." I touched his knee and gave him a flirtatious shove before I continued. One stroke. I felt the sturdiness of the hairs fighting against the blade to stay in their place. I also felt the weakness in my resistance as I fought back the desire to feel his embrace. I surveyed his face. I tried to focus, to see if I had missed a spot, but I couldn't, because all I wanted was for my blue eyes to connect with his. A glance, a moment, and our eyes held each other.

That was all it took; he had me hooked. I was beyond attracted to him, and at that moment, I ignored all thoughts that didn't involve me kissing him. Including the fact that the boy I was there to see, Scott, had been listening from the other room and had left the apartment in frustration. That didn't matter. The only thing I wanted was this man's attention, and to keep it, I was willing to do what I believed he wanted me to. I may have been only sixteen, but I had a pretty good idea what he wanted. It was what I believed every male wanted. It was what my Papaw Clyde had wanted when he touched me when I was seven years old. It was what boys had encouraged me to do from the time I was twelve years old. I knew they thought my body was a toy designed to please them. So I went along. At least I felt seen and valued, even if only for those brief moments.

"Thank you for letting me do that," I said after I finished shaving his face.

He nodded and rubbed his hand against it. "I'm going to my room. I have some lights to hang in there." His eyes lingered on me for a moment longer, as if inviting me to follow him.

"Okay," I said and blushed. But I didn't follow him. I walked back into the living room.

"Scott left," my friend, who was still sitting on the couch with her boyfriend, told me. "He's mad."

I shrugged. "I didn't do anything wrong. I was just shaving his face." I rolled my eyes. "Oh well." I didn't care about that boy. I had set my eyes on a man.

I soon grew bored hanging out in the living room. Nobody said anything when I stood back up and headed down the hall to the bedroom. As I rounded his doorway, I heard music softly playing and saw him hanging white Christmas lights around the ceiling. I stood silently, taking in every inch of him. I hoped he'd see me and stop what he was doing and come to me. I didn't have to wait long. He walked to me and embraced my waist and stared into my eyes. Then his lips met mine in a passionate kiss.

I'd never kissed a man before, not like this. It was different from kissing Papaw Clyde, or the others I had kissed; well, they had all been boys. But Gary Richard was an experienced lover who easily guided me toward his bed, where I willingly and eagerly gave myself to him.

He was kind to me afterward and invited me to come over the next week to hang out with him. That made me feel good, and I immediately told him I would. After my friend and I left the apartment, I couldn't keep the expression on my face from giving away what I'd done. She gave me a sideways glance and a slight grin. I didn't need to tell her we had sex; she knew.

And soon so did everyone else, to my surprise—my friend wasn't the type to gossip, and having sex was the norm in my circle of friends, so what had happened? The following day, I found out—another boy who lived in the apartment had been hiding in the closet that night. And he had watched.

"Did you know Thomas was hiding in the closet the other night?" I asked the next time I saw Gary Richard. His knowing look said it all.

"Well, he was, but he wasn't in there the whole time," he told me. "I asked him to stand in there because you had been flirting with me, and I just wanted to make sure someone saw you wanted *it* too. He snuck out before we really started."

I felt sick. I felt betrayed too, although I didn't know by whom. Oddly enough, I wasn't mad at Gary Richard, because in some naive way, I figured his protective reasoning kind of made sense. He was right, I did want *it*, but I also wanted him—with or without the sex.

We began spending a lot of time together, just hanging out. Though he didn't ask me to be his girlfriend, I assumed I was. He was attentive and always made me feel desirable. We would wrestle on the floor of his apartment or on his waterbed, exchange playful banter, and he would tell me how beautiful he thought I was. In awe, I consumed the stories he shared of his days as a model on the runways of bridal shows, the places he had traveled, and the many professions he had. Wide-eyed, I devoured the black-and-white image in a magazine showing him shirtless, baring his six-pack abs while standing next to a bed with a woman draped in a sheet.

I looked for his name as the model because I couldn't clearly see the face of the man in the image. It seemed surreal that I was with a man who had modeled for magazines, and part of me wondered if this was really his profession, because other kids from school who'd seen the picture had expressed their doubts. He then showed me a Polaroid photo of his toned, tanned legs straddling a woman in a chair; she was placing money in the strap of his yellow thong-like underwear. I didn't doubt it was him in this photo because I could see his face and recognized how his teeth were biting his plump bottom lip. The smiles on the women's faces were proof that other females wanted to be with him, and I'll admit that I felt a little jealous. I also wanted to be the girl he chose even more.

I didn't want to be without him. I wanted to be with him as often as I could. So I would lie to my parents and tell them I was staying with girlfriends and spend the night with him instead. We continued to have unprotected sex and party. He didn't drink, but he always made sure I had alcohol when I wanted it.

One evening my friend and I stopped by to visit. Gary Richard had an old white rag and an aerosol can on the ground next to a videocassette recorder he had taken apart to clean. He picked up the video head cleaner can and sprayed it into the rag, then offered us the rag. "Here, put your face in that and take a deep breath."

My friend grabbed it first, placed it up to her face, and inhaled. Then she laughed and said, "It makes you feel funny."

"I want to try," I said.

He grabbed the rag from my friend and sprayed more cleaner into it and handed it to me. Sitting crisscross on the floor, I placed the cloth over my nose and open mouth and inhaled the fumes into my lungs with a deep breath. Instantly, my mind took flight, drifting freely over my body and hovering there. After I came down from the high, we all laughed, then she and I tried it a few more times.

In addition to being a stripper, Gary Richard worked at a local nightclub as a disc jockey. At this point, it had become easy to lie to my parents about who I was staying with, and although I was underage, he got me into the bar with him. I loved the smooth way he talked to people—his charm had this way of reassuring them that the choice he wanted them to make would be okay. It worked really well. When the owner of the nightclub expressed concern over me being there one night, Gary Richard turned on the charm and convinced him to allow me to stay.

He brought me butterscotch drinks from the bar as I sat in the booth that overlooked the dance floor. As the night wore on, I drank and we danced. I'd never seen any of his strip shows, but based on the way he moved under those lights, I knew his fans got their money's worth.

Money was another part of his life that impressed me. If he wanted something, he bought it or somehow ended up getting it. I didn't care if he paid his bills, saved money, planned for retirement. I didn't want to learn about his credit score, 401(k), or stocks. What teenager did? I just knew I was with someone who had money, and I was sure that he would be able to buy me anything I wanted.

One evening he drove me two hours west of town to an outdoor shopping center where the wealthy people shopped. As we strolled along the sidewalk, hand in hand, we window-shopped and admired the storefront displays. At one window, I pointed at a bright red stop-sign-shaped purse that caught my eye, and sighed over how much I liked it.

"Wait here," he told me and walked into the store. Minutes later, he returned and handed me that $80 purse. My eyes widened in wonder and awe. I felt starstruck. Not only could someone afford to buy that item, but that someone was with me. I was the luckiest girl in the world! Me, the girl whose parents struggled to make limited dollars stretch as they raised four kids. Me, the girl who never got to shop or get new clothes except at Christmas or before a new school year. Now I was holding a purse that my parents could never afford. I had come so far from my humble home and life—I had found an attractive, wealthy man, and he had chosen me.

As he and I continued to stroll along, I held that purse proudly on my arm, feeling like royalty.

Money wasn't the most important thing, I knew that. But with him, I was the fortunate girl who had struck lotto gold. He was older, check! He was cute, check! He could buy me things, check! Take me places I had never been, check! He wanted to be with me, double-check!

He checked so many boxes that I couldn't think of any others that needed to be filled in, and I didn't go looking for them. I hadn't known him long, only a couple months, so I didn't know much about his past except what he freely shared. Fine with me.

I paid little attention to the boxes he had checked that I didn't necessarily want filled in. Like his previous girlfriend and the child he'd had with her. (He occasionally saw them both, though I believed it was just the child for a very long time.) Or his family life growing up—he had been raised by his alcoholic father and a sweet, loving grandmother, because his mom had abandoned him. Then one day a friend at school told me she heard he had been in prison before—for killing someone. That one got my attention. Nowhere on my checklist did I have a section for a background check.

Later that day, I asked him about what I had heard. He told me it was true that he had been in prison but not for what my friend accused him of. In his charismatic and assuring way, he explained that his crimes were related to theft. They had taken place during his teenage years when he was rebelling and had made the wrong choices. He reassured me he wasn't like that anymore. He turned his puppy dog eyes my way and said he had learned his lesson. Besides, people had unfairly labeled him a troublemaker and looked for ways to blame him, because he lived in a small town and that's what they did.

I instantly felt sorry for him, for having to endure such a hard life. I was thankful he'd found his way to a new town. I trusted what he said, and I wasn't going to judge him for a past choice. After all, I'd done plenty of things I wished I hadn't done either.

The best part of our relationship was our intimacy. I felt valued and loved when I was in his arms. But I also knew we needed to use protection. So many times I thought about it, and sometimes I would say things to him. He just brushed it off or said he didn't like the way a condom felt because it took away from his *experience*. He always reassured me that he knew when to "pull out," so I trusted him. I believed he knew best for both of us.

Over and over, we had sex without protection. Then the more we were together, he stopped pulling out. I often wondered as I lay there if I was being responsible. I knew the risk, but I didn't want to confront him, to make him think I didn't trust him. So I never said another word about it. I made a choice and didn't use my voice.

One evening an ex-boyfriend from my high school, who was now in college, stopped by my parents' house to see how life was going for me. After dating for a year, he and I had only recently broken up, and we both still cared deeply for each other. I still considered him a good and trustworthy friend, so when he asked how I was really doing, having heard the news through the grapevine that I was dating Gary Richard, I told him the truth.

"I think he's trying to get me pregnant," I confessed to him.

He listened quietly and then told me I should say something to my parents. After he left, I heard my dad's deep voice rumble through the house. "Caroline, get in here."

I'd heard that tone before, and I knew whatever my father had to say wasn't going to be pleasant. I walked into my parents' bedroom and stood stiffly at the foot of his bed.

"Your little brother just overheard a conversation between you and your friend," he said, and my stomach dropped. I clenched my fists, promising myself I was going to pummel Justin, my brother. "Did your brother hear correctly?"

I stood in stony silence, hoping my lack of reaction would discredit the truth.

My dad frowned harshly. "You're playing with fire, little girl."

He was right. I knew he was. But I was willing to take that risk. I loved the man I was with.

CHAPTER 2

LABELED: YOUNG, DUMB, PREGNANT

My finger lightly tapped the calendar page that read *April 1996.*

"No, maybe you have the dates wrong?" I mumbled and nodded my head as I frantically scanned the small corner that contained the previous months' dates. *Think, Caroline, think— what was the date of your period in March?* My finger brushed my lip, as though that would somehow make my brain work faster. *One . . . two . . .* I had missed my period by two months.

With slumped shoulders and a head too heavy to raise, I walked from the kitchen to my room and staggered toward my bed. "Please, no. Please," I begged. "If you just let me start, I promise. I promise. I won't do *it* anymore." My eyes filled with tears as I threw myself onto my mattress and stared up at the ceiling, hoping that someone or something would hear me and change what I had done.

But considering it was mid-May and there were no signs of a period, I knew. The pleas I desperately sent went unanswered, and I needed to go to Gary Richard's apartment to deliver the news.

"Mom, can I borrow the van to go see Gary Richard?" I asked.

"Okay, but don't be gone long," she replied.

As I drove away, I thought about how nice it was that I didn't have to lie about where I was going. My parents had found out I was dating him a few months prior, after my mom called my friend's house asking for me, and I wasn't there. They probably weren't surprised; I had a history of sneaking around behind their backs with my girlfriends and the boys I had been with before I met Gary Richard. But they found it odd that a man his age was interested in a girl in high school. I knew they didn't approve of him.

I brashly professed, "I love him, and he loves me." They may not have trusted him, but they accepted my explanation, or maybe they just realized that keeping me away from him would be challenging.

I parked outside his apartment and took a deep breath. Gary Richard and I had now been dating close to four months, and I knew we loved each other, but I wasn't sure if he would be ready to hear this news, and I knew I wasn't prepared to say it.

He greeted me at the door with his charming smile. I walked in and stood as stone silent as I did the night my dad told me I was playing with fire. "I think . . . I think I might be pregnant."

He placed his hand on my shoulder. "Okay," he said without hesitation, "let's go get a pregnancy test so we can find out." He didn't seem rattled or scared like I was, and as he drove me to our local Walmart, it was clear he knew what to do. His confidence calmed my nerves.

Together we faced the shelves and scanned the tower of multicolored boxes. My mind quickly tangled as I skimmed the highlights: one step, easy to read, more than 99 percent accurate, faster response … each claimed to be better than the next. How would I ever choose one?

Gary Richard reached for the cheapest box. I nodded, because by now I had learned that he didn't have the kind of wealth I thought he had when I first met him, and at sixteen, still living at home with no job, I didn't have any money either.

As soon as we arrived back at his apartment, I made my way into the bathroom, passing the same mirror I had gazed at him through only a few months before. I sat on the same toilet where he had perched himself when I had flirtatiously shaved his face. Now I was filled with fear of all the unknowns before me.

Will my parents kill me? What will the kids at school say? Am I going to have to quit cheerleading? How do I take care of a baby? So many thoughts raced through my head. I closed my eyes, hoping that would block them out.

"I am pregnant at sixteen," I muttered as I watched the now saturated stick lying on the counter reveal lines that had only moments before been invisible. It felt like the secret messages my friends and I exchanged as little girls. On our white papers we wrote words in white crayons, and then we brushed watercolors over the top of the paper and . . . voilà, the message popped up. Only this time, I was no longer a little girl—and this message wasn't innocent.

Clutching the stick in my hand, I walked into the bedroom to find Gary Richard, and as I stood waiting for him to see me, regret, shame, and fear filled me.

He placed his arms around me and pulled me against his firm chest as my tears flowed down, soaking his shirt. As terrified as I felt over the prospect of becoming a teenage mother,

I also felt relief in his embrace and knew with him this child and I would be safe.

"What will we do?" I said through my tears.

Still holding me close, he whispered, "You have options."

What moments before had felt like safety now felt as though I'd been burned. "What?" I said and freed myself from his arms. "What options?"

"I want you to have the baby, but if you don't want to keep the baby, you can get an abortion. I know of a place that does them. Or you could give the baby up for adoption."

As I listened, flames raged in my mind and charred each option he presented until only one remained untouched. Like a mama bear protecting her cub, I growled back, "No, there are no other options. I want to have this baby. We are keeping our baby."

He didn't say anything right away, and so I leaned my head back on his chest and let the tears race down my cheeks as I accepted my fate. My life was going to change. The salty tears dripped from my nose as I dragged my face away. "I need to go home. My mom told me not to be gone too long."

"Hey, look at me," he said softly as he placed his firm finger under my chin. Through the watery blur, my eyes never left his. "It's going to be okay. I love you. You can move in here. I will take care of you. I will always be here for you." His words wrapped around my emotions like a warm blanket. I needed a plan and I trusted his. Though I wasn't sure how exactly he and I would raise a baby, that didn't change my resolve.

But as I drove the van back home, I realized I was going to have to tell my parents. I didn't know how I was going to do that. But I did know one thing: I wasn't going to do that on this night.

As the school year came to an end, my sister, Blair, who was a year older, was preparing to graduate. The house buzzed with party-planning excitement as we discussed how many family and friends would come, what kind of food we'd have, how much we should buy, and what size cake we should order. This was no time for me to make my big announcement. I knew my news would kill her joy, and I couldn't bear to do that to her. She deserved to have her big day; after all, she always seemed to do things right. She made good grades. She was sensible and responsible, she worked hard, and she made her own money and was able to buy cool clothes, which I liked to borrow without asking, resulting in many heated arguments, much name-calling, and, on occasion, hair-pulling when she found out.

I never understood why she wanted to stay stuck at a boring job when she wasn't at school. I tried to work some but didn't see the need, as it consumed too much time, and hanging with my boyfriend was a lot more fun. She worked to get a car, while I thought it was easier to borrow my parents' car. She saved her money, and I thought it was smarter to ask my boyfriend or my parents to have some of theirs when I needed it. I always seemed to walk a little closer to the wild side, and she always seemed to stay closer to the practical. Though my parents never told me, "Be more like your sister," I always felt they wanted to. I loved her, but I admit I was jealous of her.

I kept my news from everyone until after the graduation and party. Now as she wrote out thank-you notes for her graduation gifts, I wrote my own note to my parents, acutely aware that I wished I *were* more like my sister. How could I tell them that the baby they were still raising was now having one? I rehearsed the conversation over and over in my head, and it never ended well.

"Mom, Dad, umm, I'm pregnant," I would say.

I'd be standing there in disgrace as I watched the tears of pain cut my mom's smooth face.

Then I'd brace myself as my dad vibrated with fury, roaring, "Caroline, how could you do this to us? Do you know how embarrassing it will be to say our teenage daughter done went and got herself knocked up? I told you this was going to happen! Get out!"

No words I practiced lessened the fear, and no amount of practice gave me any confidence that I could speak clearly to them.

The only solution I could find was to write them a note saying I was sorry for what I had done—that I'd missed my period in April and May, and the pregnancy test was positive. I wrote a cowardly note to say I was sorry I was a disappointment to them, that I understood if they didn't want me anymore, that I loved them, and I was sorry for everything.

One afternoon, now three weeks after the day I had staggered into my room, I placed a note on the wooden nightstand next to my bed. I'm not sure why I placed it there instead of somewhere my mom could have easily found it; I guess even after writing the note, I was still afraid for them to find out.

Gary Richard picked me up and we headed to his workplace. No longer working locally as a stripper or a deejay, he was managing at a pizza chain. I decided to go to work with him to be far away from the terrifying reaction about to take place at my home. As he drove, I picked up his phone, which suddenly felt like it weighed a hundred pounds, and dialed my parents' number. When my mom answered, I directed her to go into my room and look on the nightstand.

"Why?" she asked, clearly confused.

"Just go look. I left something in there." Then I hurriedly hung up the phone and waited for Gary Richard's cell phone to ring, as that was the instruction I left in the note. Not long after we arrived at his work, his phone lit up with my parents' number flashing across the screen.

I felt nauseated as I answered. I heard a sniffle, and then my mom's voice cracked over the phone.

"Caroline." It was clear she hurt too. "I read the note. Your dad and I want you to come home so we can talk about this. We love you, and we will figure this out."

I hadn't prepared to hear love on the other end of the phone. I had only rehearsed how to react to their anger and wrath, to being kicked out, to being *dead* to them, to being an object of disgust. I didn't understand why they didn't hate me or why she wasn't mad. She was filled with pure love. She didn't judge. It broke down my resolve to run. I sobbed. "Okay, I'll come home later tonight."

That evening, as Gary Richard and I drove home, we talked about me moving in with him and agreed it was the best thing. He was familiar with a lot of the assistance programs the government had to offer, since he had experienced some of this with his first child and also because of his financial struggles due to his incarcerations. He knew that since I was pregnant, the baby and I would be able to receive Medicaid to help with the medical expenses. He also knew we could get some help with food, which I was familiar with from observing my parents' financial struggles over the years.

As a little girl in the 1980s, I watched as my mom and aunt stood in the "poor folks' line" to get the free box that was filled with government cheese, peanut butter, and powdered milk. At the grocery store, I watched as my mom tore money-like sheets of colored paper from a book and handed them to the cashier. The more Gary Richard and I talked, the more reassured I was that we would be okay. He wasn't scared or running away, he had a plan to take care of us, and it didn't matter to me who was funding it.

When I arrived home, my dad had already gone to bed. My mom greeted me at the door with a kiss on the cheek and a hug. Her eyes held sadness and fatigue. "Go to bed, and we can talk tomorrow," she said. The next day, I met my parents in the living room.

"Your mom and I talked," Dad said. "We want you to stay here and raise the baby. That way we can help you while you finish school. I know as long as you live here, you can stay on my health insurance so you can go to your appointments."

As my dad talked, my mom sat and cried. I heard Dad's plan, but I silently rejected it, because I liked Gary Richard's and mine better.

"Dad, I want to move in with Gary Richard," I told him. "He and I talked, and we think it is the best thing for the baby. He is the baby's father, and I want my baby to live in the same house as him. I want us to be a family."

My dad wasn't happy with that idea. He felt that wasn't the best choice to make.

My mom wiped her cheeks every few seconds. "You want to move out?"

"Yes." Water filled my eyes to the brim.

I hoped they'd understand that my decision didn't have anything to do with them. It was about me and the life I was now responsible for creating, and that was one where I would raise my child in a home with a mother and father under the same roof. Where neither the baby nor I would ever be confused about who was the parent or the grandparent. I wanted my baby always to know I was the mother, and alongside the baby's father, I would raise the child in *our* family home.

A week later, as the calendar rolled further into June, I moved out, with the promise to my parents that I would graduate high school. As friends found out about my pregnancy, most were supportive and unfazed, like my friend who was with me the day I met Gary Richard. My friends from the cheerleading squad were kind, at least to my face, especially the day they came to the apartment with our coach to pick up my uniforms. I still considered them my friends; however, as we moved into the heat of summer and closer to the start of school, they felt distant. I understood they were busy with summer workouts, practice, and being carefree. I was living with my boyfriend with adult-life responsibilities.

One month before my seventeenth birthday, I started my senior year of high school. I might have had an adult life, but I still had a teenage mind, no matter how adult I pretended to be. Deep down, the little girl me was still naive, and I assumed people were judging me: "She is so young, she is dumb, and how is she ever going to raise a baby?" Nobody ever directly said any of this to me, but it was what I *felt* they were saying, because that was what I was secretly saying to myself. Either way, I felt their words, even the ones I was making up with each sideways glance they gave me in the hallways at school.

It happened outside of school too. I felt disgust coming from shoppers behind me as I paid for my groceries with the money the government had given me, just as my mother had. The exasperation on their faces screamed, *Another irresponsible kid, having a baby she can't support.*

When I went to the doctor's office for my checkups, I assumed my chart was labeled YOUNG, DUMB, PREGNANT. In the waiting room, I shrank under the stares of adult women carrying their growing bellies to the check-in desk with great pride, while I wished I could hide mine.

Fortunately, there was a place where I didn't have to hide. Since our school had a high number of students who were in my "condition," the school board had created a course—Pregnant and Parenting Teens—for the ten of us who were pregnant or had already become parents. By the end of the first semester, I had all the credits I needed to graduate, which made me happy because my baby boy was due in late January. I could finish high school and then focus all my attention on being a mom.

My counselor informed me, however, that if I wanted to walk with my class on graduation day in May, I would still need to attend school for one class. So I chose that class, thinking it would be a practical way to prepare for motherhood.

I enjoyed this class, the teachers, and the safety of this space. My classmates and I built friendships from shared stories because we each understood what the other faced, and we connected through our pains. Some were struggling with their babies' daddies or mamas. I called us the "High School Moms and One Dad Club." We were a tribe, and while some were going to have to raise their children alone, I quietly held on to the pride I felt knowing that my child's father would always be there.

We learned "real life" stuff that we were going to need to know in order to be good parents and raise healthy babies. I never felt labeled or judged there, except for one day when our teacher announced, "Statistically, teenage mothers have another baby two years after the birth of their first child."

In my head, I heard it like this: *You are a bunch of uneducated teens who don't know how to prevent pregnancy. You are doomed to a life of struggle with babies who will sit on each of your young hips because you are dumb.* I felt my face grow instantly hot.

My anger flared, and I wanted to prove her wrong. *That isn't going to be me,* I thought at her. *I'll show you.* There was no way I was going to be like that statistic. *I am not like them. I will not be a single teenage mother,* I promised myself. *My life won't be filled with struggle, because my baby's father will take care of me.*

CHAPTER 3

PLANS, PLEAS, AND DIARRHEA

T ap, tap, tap.

I paused from pulling the fishing line through the hole of the compact disc—a project I was working on for an upcoming bridal show where Gary Richard planned to market his work. With the television blaring in the background, I wasn't sure if I'd heard a knock at our apartment door or some sound from the television. I wasn't expecting company, and Gary Richard was at work at a local department store.

Tap, tap, tap.

This time the noise was louder as the metal screen door rattled. It was after eight o'clock on a weeknight, so I couldn't imagine any reason someone would be at the door, and any visitors we had usually called first. But I placed the CD on the table, pushed my almost-eight-months-pregnant body off the plush tan couch, and waddled to the door.

I peered through the edge of the white blind that was covered by a strategically placed sheer curtain, but it was too dark to get a clear view. I opened the door and stared into the faces of two men wearing finely pressed suits and flashing shiny badges. They introduced themselves as detectives with the police department. I couldn't imagine why they were here, so I simply stared at them in confused silence. At seventeen, I hadn't ever been in trouble with the law and had only seen detectives on the television or in movies.

"Is Gary Richard home?" one of the detectives asked.

"No, he is at work," I said.

"Do you live here?" he asked.

"Yes, I'm Gary Richard's girlfriend."

The other detective slid his hand into his jacket and pulled out a sheet of folded paper. "We have a warrant to come inside and search the apartment for stolen property."

My mind went blank. Stolen property? I didn't know what to do or say as they walked into the apartment and began their search.

I wanted to call Gary Richard to guide me. He always knew how to handle the law. He had taught me a few things too, like how fast I could drive and not get pulled over and how to shoplift. One evening while we were at Walmart, we browsed the baby section, and as we rounded a corner where the sizable highchair boxes were, Gary Richard picked up a box that had a picture of one with a blue-and-red seat and yellow tray. He placed it in the cart.

"What's that for? We don't need that yet."

He confidently told me the plan. "We'll take out the seat inside and put the items we want in it. Then I'll put the tape back over it. The cashier will scan it like normal, and we'll only pay for the seat."

My jaw dropped.

"It's perfect," he continued, "because since you're pregnant, no one will suspect anything about us buying it. We just need to go to a cashier who looks like they won't know the weight of the box, so either one who is younger and probably hasn't had kids or one who is old."

"I don't know," I stammered. "What if we get caught?" I felt torn. I knew stealing wasn't right. I remembered my mom taking my little brother, Justin, back to the store when she discovered he'd taken a pack of gum. She wanted to teach him this lesson. (Never mind that when they headed back again, he took nail polish to give to me.)

Yet his plan started to seem more sensible. We didn't have money to buy what we needed, so how else would we get it?

We walked around selecting items from the baby section, the electronics department, housewares, and cosmetics. Gary Richard arranged each item snugly in the box, and then we made our way to the checkout lane, where we scanned the cashiers and selected one who appeared to be in her sixties. We placed the box on the counter, and I gawked as she put it in her hand and paused.

A puzzled look came over her face. "This seems heavy for a booster seat; these boxes are usually light. Do you mind if I open it?"

"Not at all," Gary Richard said with great poise. He leaned in as if he were solving the mystery with her.

She grabbed a cutter and slid it across the tape that he had so perfectly put back in place. She lifted the cardboard flaps and stared inside. "What the—" She began pulling washcloths, makeup, and baby items from the box.

As I looked on, my shoulders dropped in resignation. I placed the palms of my hands over my growing belly, hoping for mercy.

But not Gary Richard. The shock he displayed was as realistic as the cashier's. "Wow! I'm glad you checked that.

We don't need any of that stuff. We just came in here to get a booster seat." Then without skipping a beat, he said, "I'll run back there and grab another one."

She believed him.

As we walked out of the store with the booster seat, I felt my resentment rise. "I will never do that again," I said, feeling tears well up in my eyes. "That was embarrassing and scary. What if we'd gotten caught? We are having a baby!"

He nodded. "I understand. The good thing is that we weren't."

I felt frustrated with him, yet I was impressed by his ability to stay calm. He was so unfazed by the outcome; he always had a plan.

Now I stood alone and speechless as I watched the detectives swiftly collecting many items around our two-bedroom apartment, taking photos, and talking to each other about different things they found.

At one point, they stood in front of the kitchen counter and stared at our large red circular-shaped phone with the words *Coca-Cola* displayed on the front.

"Was that one of the items?" one detective said.

Defensively I spoke up. "I bought that! I bought that from the store. It was a Christmas present. I think I still have the receipt."

They turned toward me, nodded to show they accepted my words, then turned away to scan the room further.

They made their way into the living room, stopped at the glass coffee table where I'd been working, and scooped up the CDs with the freshly tied lines and placed them into their evidence bag.

My head bounced with unbelief. I'd worked hard on those! How could the detectives think those were stolen?

The slam of the screen door interrupted my thoughts. Gary Richard had arrived home.

The detectives scrambled to meet him. I followed behind and leaned into the corner of the wall as they explained to Gary Richard that he needed to go with them to the police station.

Gary Richard's eyes caught mine. Just as in Walmart, he seemed calm and cool about it all. "It's okay," he told me. "I'll need you to pick me up from the station later."

As they whisked him away, I closed the door and finally let the tears flow. My hands trembled as I dialed the phone to tell my parents what had happened. I'm not sure why, exactly. Maybe because I just needed some comfort, or maybe I wanted direction from my dad, who knew about law-enforcement procedures from his years working as a deputy sheriff.

When my mom answered, I let everything spill out, feeling as though I was sharing gossip about someone else's life rather than telling the awful truth of mine.

Later the next morning, just as Gary Richard promised, he called. "Call the bail bondsman and then come to the jail to pick me up."

From the demanding rush in his tone, I knew it wasn't time to ask questions, although I wanted to. He needed me, and that meant I needed to follow his plan, so I did.

We exited the jail and made our way to the car, where I handed him the keys. As he put the car in gear, I couldn't keep quiet any longer.

"Did you do it?" Even though I asked, I didn't need the answer; I already knew. I'd seen the detectives collect the items.

"Yes, but they were *my* things. When I went to prison before, the guy held my stuff for me, and when I got out, he never gave it back. So I took them back." His words confirmed what I'd suspected. Even though he had done something I didn't agree with and knew was wrong, I found that it didn't matter. I loved him, I believed in him, and I trusted his plan for us.

A few weeks later I reported to my doctor's office for a visit. By this time, I was ten days past my due date. I told my doctor that I thought I was leaking fluid.

"I am going to induce you today," he announced.

I felt a rush of fear, excitement, uncertainty, and hunger pains. I hadn't eaten much before I came to the appointment, since I was certainly not expecting to get induced! If I had known the only thing I'd consume over the next nine hours was ice chips, I would have eaten more than the two cherry Fig Newtons I'd had in my mom's car as she drove me to the doctor's office.

I called Gary Richard at work with the news, and he came to the hospital after he stopped at our apartment to put on his EMT clothes. At the time, he was also enrolled in an EMT course at the technical college and felt that while I was in labor, it would be an excellent opportunity to do some job shadowing. Thankfully, he found his way back to my maternity room in time for the delivery of our son.

At 10:24 p.m. on February 5, 1997, I gave birth to a healthy eight-pound, six-ounce perfect-in-every-way baby boy. When they placed him in my arms, I felt love that moved me to the depths of my being. I knew I didn't deserve him, but at that moment I promised him that I would be the best mother I could be because that was what *he* deserved. I was so thankful to have him and knew that together, we would grow, me as a mother and he into a little boy and then one day a man. Though I was only a teenager and hadn't yet discovered who I was, I knew I could be who he needed me to be. He needed a mom.

A week later, I took our newborn son, Daniel, into the bathroom of the courthouse to change his diaper while I waited for Gary Richard to go before the judge regarding the items the detectives had found in our home. I laid the plastic-coated changing pad on the floor, since the restroom didn't have a table or large enough counter to use, and placed him on it. I knelt to face the creases that ran along his little feet. I put his tiny ankles in the palm of my hand, then gently lifted his legs. I pulled the soiled diaper away from his bottom, and as I turned to reach for the wipes, without warning, Daniel shot me with yellow-mustard-colored projectile diarrhea. I didn't even know that was a thing. As it landed across the front of my denim overalls, I felt my face flush with embarrassment. I looked down at the innocence on his sweet face.

He shouldn't be here, in this place, I thought. *This isn't how we should be spending the first week of his life.*

I could have stayed behind that door until the courthouse closed, but I knew I had to go back out there, or eventually, Gary Richard would search for us. I cleaned him off and put on a new diaper and his pants, then I turned my attention to the mess splattered across my clothes. Using fresh baby wipes, I washed off what I could, took a deep breath, picked up my precious son, and pushed open that bathroom door. Wet spots with hints of yellow lingered, which I tried to cover with Daniel's body. I walked down the courtroom aisle and sat next to Gary Richard. Seconds later, they called his name, and he stood. I watched him walk to the front, then fixed my eyes on the man in the black robe. The judge spoke to Gary Richard about the charges of receiving stolen property for the items at our home. Then he paused and waited for Gary Richard to give his plea.

"Not guilty," Gary Richard said.

I wasn't surprised, because that was the plan I knew he and his attorney had discussed.

The judge assigned him another court date, and we left the courthouse as a family, knowing we would soon return. This was just the beginning of building his defense against these charges.

A few months later, I made it to my graduation day. A sea of sunlight, yellow gowns, and square hats with tassels dangling filled the arena. I waited for my turn, and when "Caroline Rae" formally vibrated through the speaker system, I walked proudly up the steps, pushed forward to the center, and reached out my hand to grasp the white scroll tied with blue ribbon. As I exited the stage, my heart burst with joy that I'd fulfilled the promise I made to my dad, and I felt so thankful that Gary Richard was there holding our son in his protective arms and that they were watching me. I accomplished one of the goals for my little family's life. Now we could look toward Gary Richard accomplishing another of those goals—getting his case taken care of without going back to prison.

CHAPTER 4

MY WEDDING DAY,
HIS PLOY

"**A**re you two planning on getting married?" asked the attorney. He raised his curious eyes from the papers that contained evidence the prosecuting attorney would be presenting at Gary Richard's upcoming sentencing hearing in August, less than two months away. Gary Richard and I exchanged glances as if seeking each other's approval to answer.

We both said yes.

"Okay, that's great!" the attorney said, joy washing over his face. This was clearly the answer he'd hoped to hear. "If you get married before you go in front of the judge, I can use that to ask for leniency in your sentence, because we can show your life is different from when you committed your prior offenses. You are now a family man with a new baby and a wife."

I took in a deep breath and let my mind drift to the times as a child when I had marveled at the brides I'd witnessed gliding down the church's center aisle in long white gowns. I'd been mesmerized as they passed the flowers and ribbons attached to the end of the wooden pews and gently touched the petals sprinkled on the path with the bottoms of their heels. Theirs were elegant, regal fairy tales coming true.

Neither Gary Richard's guilt nor the contents of the case file nor the fact he had entered a plea agreement was important to me. Although the detectives had removed the items right before my eyes, innocence was all I could see. I loved Gary Richard. He loved me. I didn't need him to drop down on a knee and lovingly ask for my hand, although when I saw that in the movies or heard of other proposals, I was envious. But I understood: if I wanted my little family, then he couldn't go back to prison. He needed a ploy, and I wanted a wedding. Let the planning begin.

I knew I wanted to be married in a church. But which one? He and I hadn't attended one together, and neither of us actively belonged to any. When I was little, my parents, siblings, and I did occasionally attend a small Baptist church nestled in the neighborhood where my cousins lived. My mom suggested that I check into using that one for our wedding, because she didn't believe they would charge much to use it. I had already made up my mind that it wasn't an option, though. It was too small. I didn't want my glide to be restricted to a short walk or to cut the guest list due to limited seating.

As I began contacting prospective churches, based on size and aesthetics only, I received a similar response: "Are you a member?" That usually meant that they wouldn't rent out the church to us or that they would rent it out but for an exorbitant fee.

As I went down my list, I landed on a church I really liked. I called and was asked the same question.

"No," I replied, expecting defeat.

"Yes, we do."

I inhaled sharply, now feeling excited. Hope rose within as I listened and scribbled on my paper their prices and rules for renting. Then the real test came. Nervously, hoping I wouldn't receive an "Are you kidding me?" response with a chuckle or a "You are absurd for asking," I took the plunge. "Are you booked on August 23?" I knew it was a gamble— after all, that was only six weeks away.

"Let me check."

Her reply—without even a hint of a chuckle—turned my nerves into desperation as I whispered, "Please, *please* be available." I knew it was short notice, but time wasn't a luxury we had, since we were hemmed in by Gary Richard's hearing. The twenty-third was the Saturday before the court date.

"Yes, that date is available," the woman said, interrupting my silent pleas.

I wanted to shout with excitement but kept my voice even. "Wonderful! Can you put us down for that date?"

"Yes. I just need to ask a few questions for our records." I heard paper shuffle on the other end of the line, then she asked our names, address, and what time we wanted the ceremony.

I responded to each question without much thought as I started to wonder which reception hall we could rent now that the wedding venue was secured. I scribbled the names of places I would contact when I was finished with this call.

"Okay, and what are your ages?"

"I am seventeen and he is twenty-five."

The phone went silent. "Um, can you hold for a moment? I need to ask the pastor a question."

"Sure." It seemed odd that in the middle of our conversation, she would leave me hanging, but I was sure it was nothing to be concerned about.

After a few minutes she returned. "I'm sorry, but we won't be able to accommodate your wedding," she announced.

"What? Why? I thought . . ."

"Our pastor won't marry anyone under the age of eighteen."

Stunned and furious, I hung up the phone. "I don't even get an opportunity to explain our situation?" I yelled at the now-disconnected phone. "Um, do I get a say in the matter? Nope." I couldn't change how young I was, and I didn't understand why my age mattered to the pastor. He didn't know me or the love Gary Richard and I shared. "Well, just because you won't marry us doesn't mean you can stop us! If I want to get married, I can and I will." I plopped back against the couch cushion and crossed my arms in defiance. "I don't want to get married in your stuffy church anyway."

A few minutes later I regained my momentum. This was just one pastor with a closed mind. Surely others would be more open. I called another church and confirmed they had that weekend open and that they rented to nonmembers. Before we got further in the process, having learned my lesson, I asked if my age mattered.

"Yes," the woman said in a self-righteous tone.

I rolled my eyes at the thought of having to get married in the courthouse, but I knew that if the conversations with the churches continued to stop dead over the age question, an open-minded judge might be our only option. Still, I kept calling churches and finally found a pastor of a Baptist church who agreed to perform our ceremony, as long as we agreed to meet with him for a premarital talk.

As Gary Richard and I entered through the glass door, an older man, who wore wire-frame glasses and appeared to be in his late sixties, reached out his hand toward Gary Richard and introduced himself. Then he reached out his hand for me to shake. I appreciated his gesture. He made me feel that he was taking me seriously, as an adult.

We followed him down the carpeted hallway into what must have been his office, judging by the desk and the small couch he gestured for us to sit on. We held hands and fixed our eyes on Bob, as he asked us to call him.

"So tell me, why do you want to get married?" Bob asked.

I gazed at Gary Richard with a loving smirk. I knew why I wanted to get married, and I also understood why we *were* getting married. But I wanted to hear how Gary Richard would respond.

"I am in love with her," he said. "We have a little boy, and I want to marry her."

The fountain of love poured from my chest, as I knew this was the man I would spend my life with.

Bob looked at me. I knew he must have seen the radiant beams in my blue eyes. "And why do you want to marry him?"

I felt my cheeks grow warm. "The same reason." I softly shrugged my shoulders.

Bob then explained the details of how the wedding day and rehearsal would flow. After about an hour together, we stood, relieved and excited. We shook hands again and left.

On a limited budget, with money from Gary Richard's grandma and some help from my parents and my sister, Blair, we purchased decorations and rented dresses, tuxedos, and a reception hall. I found four matching blue prom dresses marked down to $30 for my bridesmaids. My mom ordered the cake. Gary Richard and I ordered spaghetti from a new restaurant in town—we would be able to feed our two hundred guests for $115.

Everything was falling into place—until we went to file for our marriage license. It seemed pastors weren't the only ones who had an issue with my age. In the state of Missouri, in 1997, if you were under the age of eighteen, you were unable to obtain a marriage license without parental consent.[1]

I was close, just a month shy of turning the number that would make me an official adult. Yet I needed my parents to sign, because September 25 would be too late. With the state's rejection fresh in my mind, I called my mom. "Gary Richard and I tried to get the marriage license today, and they said I couldn't unless you or Dad go there with me to sign." Not giving any time for her to process, or even respond, I begged as only a desperate teenager can. "Please, Mom, please, I need you to do this. It is the best thing for us to be a little family."

In case my long-winded pleas weren't enough to make my case, I added, "If you don't sign it now, that's okay, because in a month I can get married without your consent anyway."

She sighed. If I could have seen her face, I would have undoubtedly seen her rolling her eyes as well. "Let me talk with your dad and see what he says."

---

[1] Twenty-one years later, the law would change to further protect minors by including that even with parental consent, the other party may not be over the age of twenty-one.

"Okay," I replied, though I felt confused and frustrated. They knew we were getting married, and they knew why we were rushing. They had been actively participating in the planning, so I didn't understand what discussion needed to take place. Were they questioning if they should give their approval simply because the state was requiring them to put it in writing? As if the state knew better than we did if we should be married! I'm not sure which of my pleas sealed the deal, but the next day my mom came with us to the county office and signed.

On August 23, 1997, I glided down the aisle, past each pew delicately decorated in shades of blue. A childhood dream had come true. I stood regally in front of the church pew, putting all the grace, elegance, and joy I held into my rented off-the-shoulder, ballroom-style white gown and my heartfelt "I do." We exchanged pawn-store rings, exited the glass doors into a sea of floating bubbles our guests blew out over us, then danced in celebration at the hall for the rest of the night. My parents kept Daniel for a few nights so Gary Richard and I could have some time together as husband and wife. We couldn't afford a honeymoon, and we couldn't venture far anyway, since Gary Richard was already on probation for his prior crimes and could go only as far as the surrounding counties. So we did. We went to a water and amusement park an hour north of our town.

The morning of his hearing, I stood behind Gary Richard in the bathroom and watched him through the mirror, as I had done so many times before. Tears welled up in my eyes as I considered the possibility of the hearing not going well. "What if they send you away today? What will we do?"

He pulled me close as my body relaxed under the warmth of his breath. "They won't. I know it. We are married, and that will make a difference."

I wanted to be strong like he was, so sure of our fate, but nausea reminded me I wasn't. I sat in the courtroom pew with unease slithering down my spine as he stood before the judge for sentencing. His attorney expressed how events in Gary Richard's life had now shifted his focus, because he had a new baby, now six months old, and a new wife.

Wide-eyed, I watched as Gary Richard's probation officer stoically took the stand. "It is my understanding that Mr. Downey is currently under investigation for theft from the carpet store where he had been working."

My eyes bore into him, trying to make sense of what I was hearing.

Gary Richard's attorney objected to the statement. "Your Honor, none of that information has been previously presented, and we are unaware about what he is speaking of."

The judge agreed to strike the officer's statement. Although it didn't make sense why he would say it, I knew Gary Richard always said that officer didn't like him.

He's just trying to get him in more trouble, I rationalized to myself.

After the cloud of confusion disappeared, the judge looked out over the silent gatherers in the room. I held my breath. From the judge's throne, her poker face declared, "I am sentencing you to supervised probation."

I exhaled as warm relief flowed down my cheeks. "He is coming home," I whispered and smiled.

That was all that mattered. We could finally be a family, free from courtrooms, pleas, and detectives at our door. He would take care of me. I would take care of our home and our son. Thanks to our magical attorney and my magical wedding day.

CHAPTER 5

STAY

Less than a year after his sentencing for receiving stolen property, Gary Richard and I sat across from the public defender, listening intently as she combed through the papers. Then she looked up at Gary Richard. "An elderly customer contacted the store because her check had never cleared the bank," she said. "The concern over discrepancies in the deposits caused the store to launch an internal investigation. You had access to the deposits, and your history of theft, receiving stolen property, understandably makes you the prime suspect."

He pressed his lips together. "I think it is the manager who did it," he said. "I didn't do it, and we certainly don't have any money to prove it." He turned and smirked at me as if he had just solved the case. I didn't know if what he said about the manager was right, but his comment about our lack of money certainly was. I worked part-time, and he was on to another job in the food service industry. It wasn't enough to keep us financially secure and worry-free.

I worried. I worried about not making it to the next paycheck, as the days between them seemed to increase. Gary Richard reached out to his grandma, who sent us a check to pay a bill before the gas, lights, or water were disconnected, and I worried we wouldn't receive it on time. Financial stress was always on my mind, and so was the possibility of Gary Richard getting incarcerated. When Gary Richard received five years of probation at his sentencing, I thought I no longer had to worry about him going to prison. But the brief statement Gary Richard's probation officer had made about an active investigation at the carpet store brought all those fears back to the surface.

One afternoon, a few months after Gary Richard received his sentence, his probation officer called and requested he come to the probation and parole office for a meeting. When he arrived, the officer informed Gary Richard he had an arrest warrant. Gary Richard surrendered to the officer, who took him to jail.

I had such a sense of déjà vu when Gary Richard called me from the jail. "Caroline, can you call the bail bondsman and come down to the police station to get me? My PO told me I had a warrant, and I turned myself in." He reported it all with authority, as if this were routine.

I let out an exasperated sigh and rolled my eyes, but my stomach clenched in a knot. *What is this going to cost us?* "Okay," I said, trying not to sound worried. "What money am I going to use for your bond?" I asked him. I had more questions, like "What is the warrant for?" but I too had developed a routine—the "man I love is calling from jail" routine, which meant now wasn't the time for discussion.

"Take the money we have, including what Grandma sent to help with the bills—that should be enough. I'll get ahold of her later to have her send more."

I hung up, grabbed what little money we had, and then looked at Daniel. *No more. I'm not exposing him to any more jails.*

So I picked up the phone and called my mom and asked if she would watch Daniel, explaining the situation.

"Yes, you can bring him," she said, her tone shifting to irritation. I knew she was frustrated at the routine of this, or maybe she was irritated at the disruption of her day, as I was. I wanted to be at our apartment watching soap operas as Daniel clanged and clashed his brightly colored oversized blocks on the pale avocado-colored carpet that had left its youth behind in the seventies.

After dropping Daniel off, I parked along the curb in front of the station—another familiar routine—and stood in the lobby with the bail bondsman next to the deputy, who sat in the center of the room at a half-moon-shaped desk. I paced in short steps as I waited for Gary Richard to come out from behind a door that must have had a million locks. I stood next to him and watched him grin and firmly shake hands with the bail bondsman. Then together, he and I walked out of the heavy, silver-framed glass doors and made our way to the car.

My eyes traced the right side of his face as he pulled the car away from the curb. "What is going on? What is the warrant for?"

"You remember when my PO spoke at the sentencing and mentioned an investigation at the carpet store?"

Only too well did I remember. "Yeah, why?"

His eyes locked with mine briefly, and his mouth made a self-satisfied smirk. "They think I stole money from the deposits at the store."

I was stricken into silence as I processed what his words meant for him, for us. For me. *He couldn't have stolen money. No way! I would know if we had any, and we don't.* None saved, none tucked away. Certainly none in our checking account that was one small transaction away from being overdrawn. We had to fight against the absurdity of these accusations. Nausea rolled through me as I thought of going through the eerie uncertainty of courtroom proceedings once again. I didn't want another round with the legal system, but I knew we didn't have a choice, and I released a sheepish laugh in acceptance. "I wish we did have that kind of money."

He bobbled his head. "I know, right?"

We couldn't afford an attorney to help fight these charges in a trial, and since we had already borrowed so much money from his grandma, we couldn't ask again. But Gary Richard said he felt confident that this time he would be okay with the government-funded attorney he was appointed. She had represented him on charges in the past, and he trusted she would free him of these by building a strong defense.

I was surprised when I met her, though. *She looks so young.*

She appeared to be in her late twenties, maybe early thirties, with short walnut-colored ringlets cascading from her head. Her tiny frame supported confident shoulders as her words spread through the air, as smooth as silk. "This is a paper trail. I think it points more toward the manager too," she said, fanning the pages like a cartoon flip-book. Her smooth reassurance that the evidence they had against him wouldn't hold up at trial gave me confidence she would free him also.

As the jury selection process began, unease once again slithered down my spine. If we chose the wrong people, the beginning years of my marriage would consist of me visiting my husband in prison while raising Daniel alone. Questions from the prosecutor and Gary Richard's attorney ping-ponged across the room and snapped me back into the present.

"Do you know the defendant?"

"Have you ever testified in court before?"

"Have you ever been the victim of a theft?"

I inhaled deeply as I took in each potential juror's response, wondering which would seal their fate, then fixed my eyes on the twelve who remained to decide Gary Richard's fate and mine.

"All rise," the bailiff commanded. "This court is now in session." The heaviness of his voice pulled me from my seat while the judge moved in slow motion toward his. Sunlight streamed from the glass that stretched to the ceiling. The dark wooden banisters and spindles stood sturdy, as if they had been there, like the courthouse, since the late 1800s. His Honor announced, "You may be seated."

I leaned in to hear both sides making their opening statements. I glanced at Gary Richard's back as he sat with his hands folded on top of a wooden table that looked as old as the rails. As the trial proceeded, the prosecutor exhibited and examined images of deposit slips, bank statements, and signatures. All of the numbers and stacks of papers made the room feel stuffy. I didn't know how the jury felt, but if this information didn't have the power to change my life, I would be annoyed to sit here and listen. This case lacked the elements of an entertaining crime-scene drama. Until the witness for the defense, of all people, took the stand: the manager.

Gary Richard and his attorney felt that the manager should have been the prime suspect because he had more access than Gary Richard. The attorney called him as a witness for the defense so she could plant doubt in the jurors' minds, depending on the way the manager responded to her questioning. She wanted to lead them to at least question if the manager had more opportunity than Gary Richard.

In her fiery tone, Gary Richard's attorney unloaded a cannon of questions at him. "Mr. Smith, do all the employees have access to the cash drawer? . . . Mr. Smith, is this your signature on the deposit slip?"

To my surprise, her attacks turned his face beet red. Trembling, the carpet store manager searched for the knot to loosen his tie as sweat billowed on his forehead, and he repositioned his body, trying to get comfortable. His choppy pauses made his responses hard to hear. I wasn't sure what the jurors thought, but my mind threw out his testimony as unreliable.

After our attorney threw all her questions at him, the prosecutor finished up. With no more evidence to present, and with Gary Richard not taking the stand, the counsel rested, and the jurors left the room to deliberate. Gary Richard and I went to the café in the basement to pass the time, although I wasn't hungry.

"Could you believe how red the manager's face got?" I asked as Gary Richard prepared to take a bite from his sandwich. "I know after seeing how he reacted, there is no doubt he either did it or he knows something about it." The lack of nerves I felt as we sat there was confirmation of what we believed the verdict would be.

When the jurors returned, we shuffled back to our seats. The judge rustled papers as his forceful breath penetrated the room. "Have you reached a verdict?" he asked the jury, who replied that they had.

"The jury finds the defendant not guilty."

Gary Richard's neck bobbled back and forth, then toward his attorney. Although I couldn't see fully, I knew the corners of his mouth must have turned up. I silently sighed as my eyes flickered with joy. *We won't have to go through this anymore.*

No more allegations, crimes, or pleas. That was it. And now we could start our new life as newlyweds with a clean slate. I had already learned more about courtroom proceedings than I wanted to, and my marriage hadn't even made it into year two. I was a newlywed, a young bride, and all I knew about marriage was what I observed from the movies, or from my parents, who were now going on year twenty-two, I assumed the structure for marriage was the same—for better or worse, you laugh, love, argue, but no matter what, you stay.

I knew I was to keep our home intact and the man inside it happy. That role I had seen from the time I was old enough to understand that a woman's job was to take care of a man. During my childhood, I rarely saw my mom sitting idle. She cleaned, she cooked meals that included all the food groups, and she tended to all of her four children's needs. Rarely did I ever hear her complain or see her smile falter, even when my dad growled at what she had made. Still she served him his plate while he sat in front of the television.

"I am not eating this crap," his voice rumbled as he sent the plate flying like a Frisbee across the room. I stared at the nourishment decorating the carpet and heard my nerves tell me to stay silent as my mom bent to her knees to clean it up. My dad released frustration and anger often, but I knew he loved my mom despite the names he called her. I also knew he would provide, fight, and die for us if that was required. I saw his calloused hands bleed and heard the moans he tried to contain under his breath when he walked through the front door, his face grimacing and his legs wobbling as he desperately tried to sustain the weight of the hunched back that came from the hours of hard labor he put in to keep food on our table. I knew that was a man's role—to provide and protect his family, to fix what was broken with his bare hands, to stay.

To stay.

I never thought anything else would ever be an option for me. But one day, about two years into our marriage, while Daniel took his nap, I sat at the computer and inhaled the quiet of the room and the freedom to search the web while Gary Richard was at work. As I scanned the Yahoo home page, I moved the mouse to an area that said *Chat*, because it was flashing like the word *Open* in the window of a diner. So I clicked on it. I gulped as I recognized the flesh moving before me on the screen. I shut my eyes tightly, hoping to erase what I just saw, but when I reopened, the image was still there.

These were his private chats. My eyes examined his naked body and the descriptive words he shared with unknown females. His enhanced webcam performance was just for them.

Why would he do this? I felt hurt and nauseated. But my hurt quickly turned to anger. I grabbed the phone and dialed the first person I could think of who would be home and could get here faster than my mom. As soon as my sister answered, I blurted out, "Blair, I need you. Can you please come here and help me? I am leaving Gary Richard."

"What? Why? What happened?" I heard her fear.

I tried to talk, but words just sputtered from my gutted core. I stared into the depth of the screen, knowing I couldn't unsee or reject what was clearly there. "I can't talk. Just please come. I'll show you what I found when you get here."

I paced and fumed for the next fifteen minutes, waiting for Blair to arrive. As soon as her knock came at the door, I raced over, and with furious anticipation, I flung open the door and demanded, "Go look at what's on his computer."

Blair made her way to the fake-oak L-shaped desk. One glance at the computer screen had her gasping in horror. "Why would he do that?"

With curled lips and the bitter taste in my mouth, I hurled a response. "He is sick, that's so gross." I growled. "Done. I'm done." I'd stood by him through the arrests and trials. Everything he said, I'd believed! No more.

I tried to keep it together so I could focus on what I needed to gather before Gary Richard got home from work. While Blair watched Daniel, who had just awakened from his nap, I stuffed his and my clothes into black trash bags until they stretched. I dragged the dead weight to my car and heaved them one by one into the back seat.

Back inside the apartment, I packed Daniel's things. Anger mixed with heartbreak as I put each of Daniel's items into a bag. My baby didn't deserve a broken home. *He also doesn't deserve a cheating, lying father.*

"Caroline?" Blair's soft voice cut through my silent tirade. "Remember when you were pregnant, and you called me from school crying and accusing me of kissing him?"

My brain and pace slowed, and my lips began to quiver, as I had a sinking feeling that I knew what she was about to reveal to me. "Yeah."

Her face looked anguished, and all of a sudden it hit me. She was still hurt that I had believed his words and accused her instead of trusting she would never do that to me. "I would never do something like that to you. Why did you ever believe I would?"

"I know you wouldn't." I shook my head in wonder and disgust. "I don't understand why I believe what he tells me is the truth, and I don't know why he says things that aren't. I still don't understand why he said what he did about the two of you, even after admitting it wasn't true." I turned away. "He told me he was just trying to look cool in front of the guys because you're cute."

As I remembered his words, I felt confused and replayed all the past things he'd done. *What man lies and says he kissed his girlfriend's sister to look cool? What man goes to his best friend's house when he is out of town and makes out with his wife while his girlfriend is home and eight months pregnant? What man forwards his phone number to the home of the woman he used to date a month after he learns his girlfriend is pregnant?*

The internal replay made me want to dig a hole and hide. How blinded *was* I? How many more of his lies did I need to hear before I could see the truth? Here was the truth: he had lied to me more than once.

"I know I can't believe him," I finally told Blair, my tone expressing the defeat I felt.

Blair tucked her lips together and then nodded slowly, confirming my words were true.

I would listen to no more of his excuses. This time I could prove it, and his explanations wouldn't have the power to twist my mind and leave me feeling crazy. *If he loved me, he wouldn't hurt me like this. If he were sorry, he would stop repeating the same offense. I am* not *crazy.* The honeymoon phase wasn't supposed to be like this.

After I finished loading the car with Daniel's and my things, Blair and I stood staring at each other. She hugged me goodbye. "You can do this," she said, then she got into her car and left. She didn't say the words, but her eyes did. I think she was relieved that maybe this time would finally be the time I wouldn't *unsee* what he was doing or that I would stop feeding my family the same excuses he fed me every time I chose to look the other way.

I quickly made a plan to go back to my parents, hoping that they'd accept Daniel and me until I could figure everything out and get back on my feet. I wasn't sure how I was going to do that, and now wasn't the time to figure it all out. I just knew I didn't want to stay married to a man who cheated or who had a criminal mind. But how had I done exactly that?

I buckled Daniel into his car seat as his questioning eyes asked where we were going. Before I could respond, I heard the crunch of gravel twist underneath tires, then saw the nose of a car pull into the parking lot. Sunlight swept across the windshield as Gary Richard slammed his door; confusion washed over his face as his eyes rolled toward the piles of bags in the back seat.

"What are you doing?!" He started with a demanding tone but quickly turned his accusation into a plea. "Caroline, no, don't do this. I love you."

I spit words into his face as Daniel innocently gazed from the safety of his seat. "I saw your computer! Why would you do that? That is gross. What were you even thinking? Who does that?"

The worn-out excuses came once again. "I am sorry. I wasn't thinking. I promise I won't do it anymore. Don't do this to Daniel. Don't take him away." He begged while his body barricaded me from fully closing the door. I could feel my strength draining as his sapphire eyes began to fill with tears, so I looked away. "Caroline, babe. Look at me." He inched closer as if he knew my mind had opened for persuasion. He wasn't wrong. He placed his forehead on mine, grabbed my waist as he gently rocked back and forth as if we were dancing. "I want you, only you."

The breeze of desire carried away my resistance. He'd won again. "Okay, I will stay, but if it happens again, I am leaving. I mean it." I made the threat knowing I didn't mean it, but I believed the thought of losing me would be enough to change him. He helped me unpack the car, and we returned to our home together.

I picked up the phone and dialed my sister. "Blair, I'm going to stay."

Her heavy breath pounded my ear. "Are you sure?"

I wasn't. My thoughts pulled my eyes to the floor as my lungs expanded, and then I exhaled heavily. "Yeah, I'm sure."

As we moved into years two, three, and four, his excuses grew consistent, and my threats dwindled to nothing. I wanted to believe his version was the truth, so maybe that's why after every confrontation, I always ended up feeling bad that I had accused him.

I was standing in front of the large bathroom mirror, applying makeup before I went to the grocery store to get something to fix for supper—a familiar routine these past three years of marriage—when I heard a female voice fade into the distance. "Who was on the phone?" I demanded as I swiftly followed Gary Richard down the hallway.

I watched his face turn purposefully casual as he realized that I had overheard the voice. "Oh, that was just my boss's daughter."

I felt nauseated. I knew he was lying, but felt unable to do anything. "Um, okay." I returned to the mirror and stared into the darkness of my pupils as my mind reviewed the flashes of woman after woman he'd had encounters with. *It's just Gary Richard*, I told myself. I remembered all the times he had tried to explain his fun, flirty nature, and the jokes that drifted toward the gutter, and I thought, *It's who he is. You either love him or hate him.* I made a convincing argument and gave myself another reason to stay.

Also, he kept me confused. Either by his behaviors with other women or the way he "handled" our family finances. For instance, one evening when we'd been married three and a half years, I came home from work to him excitedly ushering me down the hall toward the door in Daniel's room. There sat a shiny new—and expensive—Jet Ski.

"How did you buy that?"

"I have been saving so I could buy it. My buddy's friend was selling it cheap." His hand proudly caressed the seat.

I blew out my cheeks as I tried to process where he found money to save and buy a Jet Ski when we desperately struggled to pay bills. Still, I saw his excitement. Then, with a half smile, I said, "It's nice." I walked away, shaking my head, wondering why I didn't feel as unfazed by our financial situation as he did.

Our marriage had me swirling in constant confusion as I struggled to love and be loved. Although our marriage wasn't easy, I told myself it was enough for me, and so was he. And I did love the way he effortlessly entertained whoever he encountered, the magnetic way he attracted fun and laughter, and the way he would get on the floor to play with Daniel. Staying together was also the path of least resistance;

maybe I made myself believe that he was enough for me. But was I enough for him? Maybe I was really the problem. I just needed to be more so that I could be enough for him.

In September 2001, four years into our marriage, we enthusiastically moved from the apartment into our yellow three-bedroom house. It was shaped like an L and located two streets away from my childhood home, where my parents still resided.

I was just shy of twenty-two and was excited about my new position as a clerk at the local hospital. For the first time, I felt mature when I went to work among older women. I was no longer a little girl floundering about at a *job*. This was a *career*. I performed my duties with integrity, worked hard, and flourished.

We still struggled with our finances, which was why we needed Gary Richard's grandmother to cosign on our home loan. But things were improving. Gary Richard was enjoying his new employment at another carpet store, and Daniel enjoyed the huge wooden playset that sat in the center of the backyard.

For the first time, our marriage was beginning to look "normal." We did what other married couples did—we made big purchases, worked, paid bills, raised children, supported each other, and loved each other. I began settling into the idea that our life was a typical married life.

This! This is why I stay, I realized one day as I looked out into the backyard and watched Gary Richard and Daniel playing together as father and son. *This is what I wanted to build with him.* As we unpacked boxes, bags, and cars to give every item a place, a huge smile took over my whole face. *This is what I wanted for my little boy—a home with two parents who . . . stay.*

CHAPTER 6

UNPROTECTED

Ding-dong.

Is that the doorbell? I tilted my head, trying to distinguish if the sound was coming from the door or from the game show on television. I was still getting accustomed to the echoes of a doorbell. Our apartment hadn't had one on the back entrance that led into our kitchen, and no guests ever rang the one at the front door—a stark contrast to our home, which we had now been in for five months.

Daniel and I had already settled into our evening routines, which for me was cleaning while listening to the television, stopping only to see if the contestant answered the question correctly. My now five-year-old was in his room, distracted by the video game he had received for his birthday just a week before.

Wonder who it is? It was after eight on a weeknight. I walked toward the door and peered through the peephole.

I didn't recognize the woman who stood on the opposite side. Heat brushed my cheeks as I felt embarrassed over having just put on pajamas. I cautiously opened the door, thankful for the security chain the previous owners had installed.

"Yes?"

"Hi, my name is Betty. I'm an investigator with Child Protective Services. There has been a call made to the child abuse hotline, regarding contact Mr. Downey had with a child, and I am here to do an investigation. Is Gary Richard home?"

I froze. *Child Protective Services? Child abuse? Gary Richard?*

Betty looked at me expectantly, but my mind couldn't grasp what she was asking. *Is he?* I didn't know—my mind felt warped. *No? Yes? Maybe? No. For sure, no.* With a distorted breath that felt like it took hours to complete, I said no. "He is at work right now but should be home soon." My lips formed an uncomfortable smile. I hoped my response would be enough for her to jot on the clipboard she held in her hand, move past the dead flowers, and get back into her car.

"Are you his wife?" she asked.

I nodded.

"May I come in and wait for him to arrive? I do need to speak with him face-to-face regarding these allegations before I leave."

Her words forced my eyes toward her clipboard as my mind rushed backward to when I was eight years old and joyously held my own clipboard. I'd cradled the stiff board in front of my flat chest, causing the silver clasp to crease the brightly colored pages I had ripped from magazines. They held images of places I would someday visit, from white sandy beaches kissed by turquoise water to the mountain peaks immersed in fluffy clouds and snow. That board had held my dreams and my future—one that didn't look like this.

The sound of Betty's clipboard broke the silence, and I snapped back to the present as she pulled a dull white card from its grasp, then held it into the gap.

I looked down at the card, which gave her name and under it her title: Child Protective Services Investigator. My thumb lowered and rose as it rubbed the state seal; clearly, her board held another version of my future, and she had no intention of leaving. "Yes, you can come in." I swished the chain to the side and opened the door wide enough to allow her to pass. As she entered, I felt the sensation of déjà vu; it was just like when those two detectives walked past me, five years earlier, at our apartment.

I closed the door and followed her heels like a puppy toward the living room. I could feel my chest pound and wondered if she could see the thumps moving the old white T-shirt I wore as a pajama top. The room seemed darker than usual, lifeless. When Gary Richard and I had first moved in, we'd discussed painting the paneling white to brighten up the space. Now as my eyes searched for comfort within those vertical lines, I wished we had.

"You have a son, Daniel, correct?"

The sound of his name pulled my eyes from the wall and back toward her. I felt the hairs on the back of my neck bristle. "Yeah, why?"

"The caller alleged that your son was present during an incident that took place in your former apartment. The allegation is that Daniel was in the room during the accused incident. Because they mentioned his name, I will need to interview Daniel to determine if he is safe in the home with his father."

My head shook, trying to erase every word I just heard. *What?* I silently screamed. *Safe! Why wouldn't he be safe?*

"What exactly does 'interview him' mean?" I said.

"I will just ask him some questions to get to know him. Like if he has pets or siblings. His favorite food or colors. If he ever gets scared. We ask these questions to begin a conversation with the child so we can decide if the child is in danger," Betty explained.

"Okay," I said as I widened my eyes to hold back the tears.

I sat there, dazed, while sickness rumbled within my belly. I thought of my sweet boy. He was safe in his room, wearing his warm Batman pajamas and in no rush to hear me say, "Hey, sweetie, it's time for bed. Turn off the game."

Betty and I stood from the couch. I couldn't see her eyes, but I imagined she was taking visual notes as she walked by the three frames nailed diagonally into the paneling and holding photos from our wedding. I hoped she was zooming in on the one of Daniel, our ring bearer, who at six months old was being pushed down the aisle in a stroller and wearing the penguin tux that matched his daddy's.

"Hey, sweetie," I said to Daniel, who was tucked deep into the sky-colored beanbag underneath his loft bed. He looked up and took in Betty's presence as the light from the television screen flashed across his cheek. "This is my friend Betty. She wants to meet you and see what cool stuff you are doing in here."

"Hello," Betty said with a soft voice. "What game are you playing?"

Daniel responded excitedly, "Sonic the Hedgehog."

"That game sounds fun. Will you tell me about it?"

I smiled wide and tiptoed backward out of his room. I knew that question was music to his ears and that Betty was going to be in there a long time. Daniel was a talker.

He especially liked to give you every detail of every character and their special powers in the games he played or shows he watched. Once at day care, the owner's husband timed him to see how long he would talk if nobody stopped or interrupted him. Two hours later, her husband felt it was time to change the subject.

I sat on the couch alone, closed my eyes, and inhaled deeply. Images of me pushing my pregnant body off the couch drifted through my mind like sand through an hourglass. Back then, my son was protected safely within my womb. Now, according to a woman I didn't even know, he wasn't protected. The sound of Betty's feet brushing the carpet startled me.

That was fast. I examined her raised chin and slight smile for a clue on how the conversation went, since she had only been in there about ten minutes.

"He is a sweet boy," she said and then chuckled. "He certainly likes to talk."

I nodded and joined her with my own chuckle. "Yes, he does."

"Mrs. Downey, Daniel doesn't appear to be in danger or feel unsafe. He is very talkative."

I nodded again.

"Usually children are more withdrawn and harder to engage in a conversation when there is abuse."

"Okay." I hugged my body, feeling relieved and wondering if the ink on the white paper attached to the clipboard said, *This child is safe.* I tried to make it out, but between the angle she held it at and the water that pooled in my eyes, I saw nothing but a blur. But I thought I saw the words *Home is clean and nicely decorated.*

"Because this is an active investigation, Daniel will not be able to have contact with his father until there is an official determination made on the case." Her face was set firmly. "If you can't make sure that won't happen, we will need to remove him from your care and place him in the children's home until the investigation is complete."

I could feel the veins start to throb in my neck. *You are not taking my son away from me.*

"I hope you understand that I've encountered too many women who choose their spouses or boyfriends or companions over their children and knowingly leave their children unprotected. I just need to ensure that doesn't happen with your son."

I understood, but still, I felt attacked. *She just said kind things about us, and now she's saying this? How can she think that about me?* I heard the disdain in her voice, and like a mama bear protecting her cub, I aggressively struck back. "As his mother, I will do anything to protect him, and there is no way he is going anywhere away from me. I will follow your instructions and keep him away from his dad until this investigation is complete. You have my word."

"Can you call Gary Richard at work to see when he will be home?" she said.

I did as she asked. "Gary Richard, there is an investigator with Child Protective Services here. She needs you to come home so she can speak with you. She won't leave until you do."

"What?" he stuttered. Gary Richard always knew the words to say, the ones that made things go his way, so his response startled me. "I'm leaving now."

I informed Betty that Gary Richard was on his way home, then we sat silently and waited. I found myself watching the wall clock's hand as it moved from dash to dash at a halting pace. I grew envious of its routine and how it knew what to do. I wanted that too. I wanted to tell Betty goodbye. I wanted to go to my little boy's room and watch him climb up his ladder, plop under the covers, and pull them up to his neck, leaving all ten of his toes exposed. I wanted to place my arm over his belly and nestle my face into his neck as we recited the same prayer I had offered since I was a child, "Now I lay me down to sleep . . ."

"Will you and Daniel stay here or will Gary Richard?" Betty's voice brought me out of my trance.

Her words made it very clear: she wasn't the only one leaving this house tonight.

I choked down the sour contents rising from my stomach. "Gary Richard doesn't have anywhere else to go. His family doesn't live around here. So Daniel and I will go stay with my parents." As Betty looked on, I called my mom and briefly explained the situation. Her gasp didn't make me feel better, but I appreciated that she immediately agreed to allow us to stay with them.

I got off the phone feeling devastated and mad. Mad at whoever called this accusation in and disrupted my family in the blink of an eye. Outraged that the state had the power to take my child away. And distraught, thinking that if any part of this was true, it would mean I failed as a mother because my son had truly been unprotected.

The glow of lights turning into the drive illuminated the mini blinds for less than a second before they turned back to off-white. I heard the clangs of the chains as the garage door lifted, then slammed shut along with the car door.

Hinges squeaked as Gary Richard stepped heavily through the kitchen door. As he reached the carpet and stopped at the end of the couch, everything went silent.

His cheeks were red, as if he had been running.

Betty motioned for him to sit down, and she and I scootched down to make room, although there was plenty. She explained to him the allegations and the investigation process, and I couldn't take my eyes off him.

Like I was playing a game of I Spy, I examined every inch of his face, looking for clues that might reveal the mystery of what he was capable of. I saw his lips twitch, heard the flow of his gasps, and watched as his brow furrowed, lowered, and rose. I observed the speed of his head shaking in apparent disbelief as his lids lubricated the blue of his eyes, and the moisture that appeared on his cheeks as his eyes leaked. I got no answers from all of my sleuthing, and I could no longer give it any more focus because I had to turn my attention back to my little boy.

I excused myself and headed into Daniel's room.

Betty waited with Gary Richard on the couch as I quickly packed items for Daniel and me while he continued to play his game. "Hey, sweetie, it's time to turn off the game. And guess what? Tonight, you and I are going to go stay at Grandma's!" I tried to make it sound like an exciting adventure. "Daddy just got home, and he is talking with my friend."

"Cool! Okay," he said and turned off the game. We walked into the living room as Gary Richard and Betty stood.

"Hey, buddy," Gary Richard said to Daniel.

"I told him we are going to go stay at Grandma and Grandpa's house," I informed Gary Richard.

He locked eyes with Daniel. "You have fun and tell them I said hi. Daddy has to go away for work for a few days, so you be a good boy for your mom, okay?"

Daniel nodded. "Okay."

Gary Richard stretched out his arms for Daniel to give him a hug goodbye as Betty and I watched.

"Okay, Daniel, time to go," I said, trying not to let him see me cry. We headed to my parents' house, two streets over.

Betty had made it clear that Gary Richard and I weren't to have any contact with each other either, and any conversations he and I needed to have about our shared finances would require her approval first. She also explained that the investigation could range from a week to thirty days, depending on when all the official interviews for the investigation took place.

For the next ten days I complied with Betty's demands, although I didn't like not knowing what was taking place at my house or how Gary Richard was. While Daniel was doing well, enjoying time hanging out with Grandma and Grandpa, his questions showed that he missed being home. "Mommy, when will Daddy be home?"

"Soon, baby. He is still out of town working." I hated lying to my sweet, innocent boy, but I also couldn't expose him at that age to the truth.

"Mommy, when can we go home? I want to play in my room."

"Soon, baby, soon."

I wasn't sure when *soon* was, but I was thankful that to a five-year-old, just speaking that one syllable was enough.

I continued to work at the hospital, abided by the rules of having no contact with Gary Richard, and called and spoke with the caseworker's voicemail multiple times for status updates on the investigation.

One afternoon, five days after our forced separation, my phone rang. The caller ID told me it was Betty. "Mrs. Downey?" a low tone said, catching me off guard. "My name is Dave. I work with Betty, and I am also working on the case. I conduct the interviews for the children, and we will need you to bring Daniel in so we can meet with him."

"Oookay," I responded, drawing out the word as I tried to understand.

"I do want to let you know we videotape all of our interviews," he stated, as tingles of dread began to crawl over my skin. I covered one eye with my palm and pressed the tips of my fingers deep in my scalp. I didn't understand any of this process. I knew the design was to protect children, but how was my child in a situation where he needed this kind of protection?

Dave explained how the videotape was to protect the child because of the transparency of the conversation. He told me they never ask a direct question about the allegation so as not to lead the child or plant thoughts in his head. He assured me they would just talk to him, just to make sure he was safe.

The next morning, pain seared my heart as I clutched Daniel's hand and led him toward the door of the children's advocacy center, a place I didn't know existed until twenty-four hours before.

"This is a place where kids go to talk," I told Daniel, keeping my voice calm and soft. "I told them how smart you are, so they want to talk with you."

He bobbed his head and grinned.

We entered a place where no child should ever have to go, and as they kindly ushered Daniel into a room filled with coloring books, toys, and a tripod holding a camcorder, I wanted to attack every person who had ever harmed a child.

I waited in a chair along the wall outside the room for what seemed like hours, although it only ended up being twenty minutes. I wrapped my arms around myself and fixed my eyes on the floor. My legs rocked, and I wondered how Daniel was. *Is he coloring? Is he confused? Is he comfortable or scared of the man in the room?* My mind furiously shifted between guilt—*He shouldn't be here, no child should*—and shame—*I am a bad mother. I can't even protect my little boy from this nightmare, and good moms protect their babies.*

"Mrs. Downey?" Dave spoke my name softly, breaking into my thoughts. His tone was soft and kind, as though he was trying to calm the storm in my head.

I pulled my eyes from the floor and looked at him.

He sat in the chair beside me. "Before we bring Daniel out, I need to explain what happened. I told you on the phone that we avoid asking the kids direct questions about the allegations."

I nodded my understanding.

"Your son is very talkative, so much so that no matter what I asked, I couldn't get him pulled into our line of questioning. He would go back to excitedly telling me about the Power Rangers, his favorite superheroes, and playing with his friends outside. Because of this, I did have to ask him about his father directly. I am sorry."

I gasped as if he'd stolen air from me along with the innocence I felt that question stripped from my son. Tears dropped down and spotted my jeans, and Dave handed me a tissue. I shook my head as I tried to imagine how confused or scared my little boy must have been when this man sitting beside me asked him if he had been touched inappropriately by his father. Did Daniel even understand?

"You said you wouldn't mention his father," I said, feeling betrayed.

"I know, and I am sorry. I tried everything to avoid it."

Everything, really? I went silent and turned my eyes back to the floor. I couldn't respond; I didn't know what else to say.

He left to retrieve my son.

I clutched my little boy's hand, worried about him. His face was like stone, and he was unusually quiet. I quickly led him outside. He gripped the fur of the stuffed baby tiger they had given him. He climbed into the passenger seat, since he had reached the state's age and weight requirements, and buckled himself in.

As I drove, I thought about times I had protected him throughout his young life. I'd covered outlets, I'd blocked stairs, I'd protected his skin from bugs and sun damage. Why couldn't I protect him from this? Was I the kind of mother who could sense all the dangers in the home? Would I recognize them if they were exposed? With every glance at him and the road, I questioned myself. Though he was quiet, he seemed okay, but he always did. I knew he was silent, but I also hadn't asked him any questions because I didn't know what to ask. *Do you want to talk about what happened? Are you hurt or confused?*

Six blocks from the building, I got my answers. Tears slid like rain down his innocent cheeks. I pulled the car into an empty parking lot and stretched my arms around him. With every squeeze, I hoped he would hear the words he needed me to say. The ones to help him make sense of all the things that felt wrong, the ones I couldn't speak because all I could do was silently scream, *I am sorry, so very sorry. I didn't protect you from this.*

"I love you," I whispered as I pressed my lips into his hair.

"I love you," he said softly.

Less than two weeks after the investigations began, the investigators were unable to verify the allegations, and the caseworker told us to go back to normal. I knew she meant to go back to living together without restrictions, which Daniel and I did, but what was normal? I couldn't just forget what had happened—what they had put my family, and my innocent child, through. *How are we supposed to go back to "normal," carrying the emotion and memories of things that aren't normal?* I wanted to ask her. Her life hadn't changed. Nobody had uprooted Betty's or Dave's lives. But they'd done that to mine, to my family's. They'd placed suspicions there that wouldn't just disappear now that they said everything was okay.

"You ready for your surprise?" I said excitedly to Daniel as we stood inside our garage after ten days of being away.

He clapped his hands and bounced up and down. "Yes! Yes!"

I turned the knob and pushed open the door that led from the garage into the kitchen. Daniel's smile took over his face, and he darted into Gary Richard's open arms, knocking him a little off balance. They rocked side to side, grinned, and laughed together.

Gary Richard brushed the corners of his eyes. "Look what I got you." He pointed to a shiny red bike with black handgrips and flame stickers on the frame.

Daniel's eyes grew wide and he raced to it.

"Close your eyes," Gary Richard said to me as he pierced me with his baby blues. He grabbed my hand. "Keep them closed," he playfully commanded as he ushered me across the carpet. When I heard the creak of the floor, I knew we were standing in the bedroom. "Open them."

I took in the tranquility of the lavender colors flowing around the room, from the fluorescent white comforter stitched with fields of flowers across its queen-sized surface to the matching purple curtains hanging like clouds over the windows.

As he wrapped his strong arms around me and pulled my back deep into his chest, my head nestled into his neck, and I felt "normal." This felt safe.

"Babe, I am sorry this happened," he whispered into my ear. "I would never hurt our son. I would never hurt a child like that."

I could feel the heat from his breath as I ingested his truth.

"This whole thing is just people trying to stir up crap and get me into trouble."

I knew he would never hurt our son, so the only thing that made sense was believing the people who made the allegations were indeed out to get him. If they were telling the truth, then their allegations wouldn't have been "unsubstantiated."

As we swayed in triumph, holding each other, I closed my eyes and thought of all we'd endured over the past week. I exhaled in relief that my family was safely back together in our home, silently vowing that never again would my husband be accused or my child be in a situation where he was considered unprotected.

CHAPTER 7

HOW DID I GET HERE, AGAIN?

"I want to have another baby," I declared to Gary Richard's profile as I stood looking into the garage from the kitchen. I was now twenty-three. We had just celebrated our first anniversary of homeownership and five years of marriage. Although Child Protective Services had been at our home only eight months before, things since then were drama-free, with no unexpected guests at our door and no pending court cases. We had settled into our home. And I figured this was a good time to add to our family.

"Okay, if that is what you want," he responded as he tinkered with the tools on his workbench.

"Yes, it is. The doctor's office said that the longer I've been receiving birth control shots, the harder it may be to get pregnant, so it might take a little while after I stop."

Not losing sight of his tools, he nodded.

I had been on the Depo shot for five years. When Daniel was born, my provider recommended it as one of the safest forms of birth control. I also appreciated how it aided me in ripping that high school "second child within two years" statistical label away.

Gary Richard was setting up the last details for a Halloween party we were hosting. I had taken a few days off work to get ready for the party and to see the doctor for my annual wellness exam. The house was now ready to host our guests, and knowing we would soon be trying for our second child was all the more reason to celebrate.

The party soon got underway, as costumed guests arrived ready for some adult Halloween fun. Bright beams of lights chased each other across the cold gray concrete floor as the music from Gary Richard's disc jockey speakers bumped and rattled the homemade cobwebs that stretched over the windows of our two-car attached garage. Ghosts, clowns, and characters from "Little Red Riding Hood" moved like zombies and did the moonwalk as they danced to Michael Jackson's "Thriller."

Gary Richard wore banana-colored vinyl pants with suspenders that rested over a bright red shirt bearing the words *Slim Jim*. He also donned a hat that resembled a tree trunk.

I wore sheer hot-pink harem pants with a matching hat and a veil that dangled down over my face and cupped my chin.

As our bodies moved in sync, Gary Richard's eyes traced the V-shaped fabric that outlined my breasts while his hands glided along my bare midriff. Together we dominated the dance floor, and the vodka ran through my blood and blurred out anyone else around us.

We had the time of our lives as laughter, chili dogs with nachos, and alcohol circulated around the room well past midnight.

"Your party is the best," my cousin said with his glass raised, walking to the door.

"You know it. See you at our next one on New Year's Eve," Gary Richard said into the microphone.

The way Gary Richard and I entertained guests felt right, and I planned for us to host parties every Halloween and New Year's Eve for the rest of our lives. We were a good team.

That November, for the first time in five years, I didn't go to the doctor's office to receive my birth control shot, and a month later, we clinked our glasses together and kissed to ring in 2003. It was time to grow our family.

As we moved through January, my cycle came and went, along with a short, spotty one in February. It had now been four months since our pre-Halloween-party conversation about having a second child. A week later I turned to the planner in my purse and strummed my fingers over the word *March*. Although it had only been three months since I stopped birth control, with each month that passed, it felt as if *years* had passed instead. I folded my arms and silently shouted, *How much longer?*

By late March, I realized I had missed my expected start date, so I went into my bedroom and pulled a pregnancy test from the stack I had stored in the corner of my dresser drawer. I went to the bathroom and nervously but impatiently took the test.

"I'm pregnant," I said as I rushed into the computer room, where Gary Richard was sitting. I waved the urine-covered stick like a flag in the air.

The corners of Gary Richard's mouth stretched up as he adjusted his glasses and moved in for a closer look at those two lines. He wrapped his arms around my waist, and I raised one arm to keep the stick in the distance while placing my other around his neck to maintain balance. "That didn't take long," he said as we swayed.

I chuckled. "I thought the same thing."

We had just entered spring, the season of new beginnings, where buds turn into blooms. As new life came to earth again, I felt thankful that I was here, again, growing a child within the safety of my womb. And after a few weeks, I noticed that my pregnancy was progressing smoothly and I didn't suffer from morning sickness as I had with Daniel. I daydreamed about the life inside of me and the shades of green I would decorate the nursery in if this baby was a girl. The walls would be painted in shades of mint, with hunter-green leaves and vibrant red ladybugs stenciled throughout.

By six weeks, I was feeling confident and happy. But one day while I was at work at the hospital, I took a bathroom break and saw blood in the toilet. I jolted to my feet.

This isn't good! I shouldn't be bleeding. Something is wrong.

I raced out of the bathroom as water filled my eyes.

My coworker Regina realized something was going on and rushed to my side. "Are you okay?"

"I'm bleeding," I whispered, fighting against the pressure to start hyperventilating.

She placed her hand to her mouth in shock. "Call the doctor."

I called, and the nurse instructed me to come right away to the office for tests. I was grateful that the doctor's office was in the hospital where I worked, so I only had to walk there.

As soon as I walked into the office, a nurse met me and escorted me back to an exam room, where the doctor performed a transvaginal ultrasound on me.

"Do you see this area?" the doctor explained as she pointed to a dark blob on the screen.

I nodded.

"This is where I believe the bleeding has come from." Her finger slid along the fuzzy black-and-white ultrasound images. "This is where the placenta attaches to the uterine lining. This area could indicate it is pulling away. We will monitor it, get some labs. This could be your body terminating the pregnancy. We will need to wait to see what happens."

My eyes stretched to take in the magnitude of what she said and to barricade the pain in my heart. My mind revolted against my body as it silently screamed. *How do you terminate the very thing you wanted?*

I took the white papers from Nurse Sara's hand. They told me what to expect during a miscarriage. Her eyes smiled softly. I knew she was trying to console the ache she saw in mine. I liked Sara. I always enjoyed our small talk conversations at my son's grade school, where she also worked as a nurse.

"If you lose the baby, it will more than likely occur over the weekend," she said. "So you will need to go straight to the obstetrics unit so they can be sure your body has removed all the tissue."

I wanted to run far away from her and her words.

I dragged my body back to my office on the first floor, closed the door, slumped in my chair, and fought back the tears. I placed the beige phone receiver to my ear, pressed nine to get an outside line, and then dialed the numbers to Gary Richard's cell phone.

"Hello." The sound of his voice blocked mine and caused tear-shaped pain to drip from my chin. "Caroline, hello."

I swallowed to lubricate my dry throat. "The doctor thinks I am going to lose the baby." Through sobs, with a cracking voice, I explained the details.

He listened, sounded supportive and sad. "I love you."

"I love you too," I whispered with a breath that in a different context could have been mistaken for being seductive. "Gary Richard, what if this is our little girl? I don't want to lose our daughter."

"I don't either."

Not that gender would have changed the ache I felt nor lessened the grief of a child lost, but from the moment I had gotten pregnant, I had wished for a baby girl.

Regina entered the office, expanded her arms as if they were taking flight, and wrapped my trembling body in her arms, like a towel after a shower. Drops fell from my nose and spotted her hunter-green scrub top, and I sniffled, trying to get control of myself. We didn't speak. I didn't need words of comfort. I just needed to cry.

Over the weekend, I lay on the couch to rest and watched more television than usual as Daniel played in his room and Gary Richard tinkered outside or in the garage. Weekends usually went by so fast, but with every trip to the bathroom, it felt like this one would never end.

"Please, no, please no," I silently begged each time I lowered the waist of my pants just above my knees. And each time I found no trace of blood, I exhaled in relief. "Thank you," I prayed.

On Monday, I reported to the doctor's office for another lab test. Then began another period of wait. Wait to see if I continued not to bleed, wait to see if bloodwork would show numbers that were increasing, wait to see if my body would hold on to the life attached inside.

After seven days passed, my doctor announced that the risk of a miscarriage had diminished. "I believe the bleeding came from the pooling of blood between the lining that surrounds the baby and the uterine wall. Since you have not had further bleeding, and all our tests show you are at a low risk, I am going to treat this as a normal pregnancy."

I inhaled the sweet smell of the room's sterilized equipment. I felt as though spring flowers were growing within my chest and pushing up my cheeks. I looked at Gary Richard. As he wiped the corners of his eyes, I knew flowers were blooming in his chest too.

A few months later, in late June, Daniel, Gary Richard, and I focused on the fuzzy ultrasound screen as the technician glided the warmed gel across my round belly. She stopped over different areas that I could not identify but trusted she could. She explained what organs she was measuring or checking for, then she stopped.

"Do you want to know your baby's sex?" she asked, smiling.

"Yes!" I said, holding my breath.

"It's a girl."

Smiles fell across our faces as we all looked at each other.

"You're going to have a baby sister," Gary Richard announced as he wrapped his arm around Daniel's shoulder.

Daniel bounced and clasped his hands in front of his chest as his eyes lit up like the sky on the Fourth of July.

"We already know her name," Gary Richard said to the technician, his voice sounding proud.

"You do?" She smiled and lifted her eyebrows.

"Yes. It is Ember. My wife has loved that name for years, and we knew if this baby was a girl, that would be her name."

I nodded, feeling so loved by Gary Richard at that moment.

"Timmmber," Daniel shouted.

Laughter erupted around the room at Daniel's confusion.

"No, not timber, like they holler when a tree is falling," Gary Richard said as he rustled Daniel's hair. "*Ember*. Your sister's name will be Ember."

Walking out of the appointment, everything about my life was *right*. I had an amazing son and would soon welcome the beauty of a daughter. My husband was more involved at home than ever before. He had a new job selling campers, which he seemed to enjoy, and was coaching our son's Little League baseball team. We were a family, living life together, sharing our days. I looked back at Daniel as he climbed into the car and then at Gary Richard as his hands gripped the steering wheel like a clock with both hands at noon. *Everything is going to be great from now on*, I thought and smiled as I buckled my seat belt.

Ring, ring, ring.

Gary Richard grabbed his phone and got out of the car. Daniel and I watched from the car windows as Gary Richard walked the length of the car over and over, nodding into the phone, then got back in and tossed his phone in the cupholder. The engine rumbled as Gary Richard turned the key. He reached out toward the dial of the radio and rolled the volume up so music projected from the speakers in the back, where Daniel was sitting. His expressionless eyes locked with mine. "That was my boss," he said in a low tone. "He told me not to come back. They are firing me. They found out about my felony record."

"What?" I shouted.

"They ran background checks on all the employees because there have been items missing from the store."

My tears, which moments earlier signaled happiness, now betrayed despair. As we drove away, I sighed and questioned why today, of all days, the joy couldn't stay? Internally, I shook my head, trying to determine if I was angry with him for lying about having a criminal record or at his employer for discovering he had one. Externally, I stayed calm, knowing Daniel was watching from the back seat. I hoped the music had drowned out Gary Richard's and my adult conversation.

How did we get here? The place where joy can't stay? The place where job loss magnifies the weaknesses in our financial management plan? We didn't have savings to fall back on, and Gary Richard's grandma had bailed us out enough throughout the years. We couldn't ask to borrow money that we never paid back. I knew Gary Richard would get another job, he always did, but that still meant we had to wait for a paycheck even though the bills wouldn't stop rolling in.

And we were already behind. Our financial plan hadn't changed much over our almost six years of marriage. Budgeting was far from our minds, and we routinely spent more than we made, just as we routinely took out payday loans to cover us until the next payday. Then when payday came, I figured out which utility bill I could call to make a payment arrangement on and extend out the disconnect date. That freed up enough cash to pay the minimum payment to the payday lender and then search for another lender to borrow from to keep us afloat until the *next payday.*

I felt suffocated by our lack of choices in lenders and by my stupidity, because I knew better than to use payday loans.

We both knew they carried astronomical interest rates, but they were our only option due to our poor credit. With each loan, we always intended to pay it back in full by the next payday. But we never did. The loans were a means to an end, and a means that would never allow our ends to meet.

We were good at one thing, though—covering it up. Nobody except Gary Richard and me knew how dire our financial situation really was, because those around us saw smiling faces, a home filled with decor, and a manicured lawn. They saw a couple who hosted parties, went on trips, and wore beautiful clothes. And four months later, they watched our family grow.

It was the evening of Wednesday, October 22, and I was out on the front porch stretching cobwebs around the columns for our Halloween decorations when my stomach felt as though someone had balled their fist up inside of it. I stepped back and placed the palm of my hand over my belly. *Is that a contraction?* I shook my head. *No, can't be. It's too early.* I finished decorating and went inside to get ready for bed, knowing I had to be up by five in the morning for work.

About thirty minutes later, though, my stomach tightened again. And again after another thirty. I dozed in and out of sleep, trying not to move too much so I wouldn't wake Gary Richard. In a few hours, he had to be at work at the machine shop, a job he had gotten a few months after being fired, and there was no point waking him if I wasn't in labor. I stared at the numbers glowing on the clock, calculating how much time had passed since the last pain.

"Twenty minutes," I mumbled.

When the next twenty came, I hit the button on the alarm to turn it off and got up. I figured I would at least start to get ready for work, as I was still not convinced I had gone into labor. Standing in the mirror, applying makeup, though, I noticed the pain was now coming ten minutes apart.

I headed toward the kitchen and grabbed my keys off the counter, knowing that once I got to work, I could go to the doctor when the office opened at eight.

"O-Oh!" I groaned. My legs felt like noodles as my knees went toward the floor. The pain intensified and came consistently.

I sucked in air so rapidly it sounded like I was hissing. After it passed, I sighed. "Ahhh."

I stood back up and rushed out the door, knowing it took ten minutes to get to work, and that was how long I had until the next contraction.

As soon as I arrived, I headed directly to labor and delivery. The doctor came in not long after and checked on me. "You're definitely in labor," she said.

I called down to my office to let them know, and then I called my husband. "Gary Richard, I am in labor!"

"Okay, I just dropped off Daniel at school. I'll head back to get him and then be on my way to the OB." His voice sounded excited.

"Please hurry." I groaned as I watched the line squiggle across the screen, showing the intensity of my contractions.

Gary Richard, Daniel, my mom, and my sister all arrived at the hospital before ten to wait with me.

I remained in labor the next few hours, and at 12:07 p.m. on October 23, 2003, I gave birth to a beautiful, healthy seven-pound, two-ounce daughter named Ember.

The nurse wrapped her body in a white cotton blanket and laid her in my arms. My eyes traced every inch of her rounded, perfect face. Delicately I pressed my lips to her forehead and became instantly addicted to the freshness of her scent. I raised my eyes to look at Gary Richard, and we both smiled. I wasn't sure exactly what he was thinking, but I whispered, "Our little girl is here."

He nodded, leaned in, and pressed his lips firmly into my head.

With his touch, I felt the peace of his protection cascade around me. The parched landscape of our finances was the furthest thing from my mind, though not much had changed. We were far from being free from our financial struggles. Even though Gary Richard had started a new job, our bank account was still bone dry. Yet when I stared at my daughter, my son, and my husband, none of that mattered. I felt our wilderness had blossomed into a lovely garden, and I had all the nourishment I would ever need. My family was complete.

Three months after having Ember, I went back to work. A week later, Gary Richard and I decided that I could stay home with Ember and only work a few days a week at the hospital to save on the amount of money we would be paying for day care. I was ecstatic at the opportunity to stay home with Ember. I didn't think about any impact it would have on anything else.

Ember spent the days alongside me while I watched television; when I wasn't holding her, she would sit in her swing, gazing intently at its legs as I cleaned the house. I wondered if the steady way they slid in and out of her view made her feel safe when I wasn't around. Or if the ritual way we played—lunchtime car rides to the McDonald's drive-through, taking Daniel to and from school—brought her a sense of comfort that allowed her to explore and learn. I knew my children needed routines, a roof over their heads, and time with their parents to develop well and thrive. So, day after day, I hoped my decision to stay home with them would outweigh our financial struggles. That their trust in me to be there, to put food on the table at dinner or wrap oversized towels around them when they got out of the bath, was worth more than full-time hours at work. So we fell into our routine, and Gary Richard did too.

He consistently worked at the machine shop, and we paid what we could. But we couldn't keep up on the mortgage; the payments grew each month because of its adjustable rate. We got further behind throughout the year following Ember's birth, until finally we received a letter indicating that our home would be going into foreclosure unless we paid the thousands of dollars we owed the bank.

I slid down the paneled wall as tears cut down my cheeks. "Why would they do this to us?" I yelled. "They can't take our home away, can they?" There had to be another way.

I dragged my feet toward the phone and dialed the bank's number. When a high-pitched female voice answered cheerily, my eyes rolled. *What are you so happy about?* "I would like to speak with Tom," I demanded.

"One moment, please, let me see if he is in. Can I tell him who is calling?" she said as if her head was bopping side to side like a cheerleader.

I shook mine in irritation, wishing I could go back to when I excitedly waved pom-poms under those Friday night lights that brightened with school spirit, and when some games were over, the only loss I had to face was up on the scoreboard. "It's Caroline Downey."

She put me on hold, and for the next few minutes I listened to instrumental music.

Finally, I heard a click. "Hello, this is Tom."

"Tom, it's Caroline Downey. Today I got a default letter on the house. Is there anything that can be done to stop this?" My agitation with the receptionist's voice transformed to deep sadness.

"I am sorry, Caroline, but unless you can come up with the money to bring the mortgage current, there is nothing we can do to help. You don't qualify for a loan modification."

I hung up the phone and sat defeated on the floor and rested my cheek against the wall. *What are we going to do?*

A familiar phrase drifted through my head. *Don't back away, stay in there.* I was fourteen, and our family had just finished watching *Rocky*. My siblings and I threw boxing punches into the air. Then my younger brother Justin, who was thirteen, decided he wanted to throw some toward me. I felt the air brush my face, and I backed up in fear.

"Stay in there," my dad coached from his recliner. "He is expecting you to back away. Don't move."

I nodded and whispered to myself, "I can do this. Don't back down." I extended my arm, and Justin's teeth ran straight into my fist.

That's what I need to do now. Not back away.

I raised my head and took a deep breath, feeling as powerful as I had in that moment ten years before in my parents' living room. I knew I could save our home. If Tom could just see me, he would see in my face how much it meant to me, and then he would do something. I knew he could fix what we broke.

The following day I asked my mom if she would keep the kids. I didn't tell Gary Richard where I was going because I knew he felt hopeless at the thought of losing our home, and I didn't want to add to it if my trip wasn't successful, especially while he was at work. Then I drove to the mortgage company, unannounced but unwilling to back down.

Closed for lunch. My eyes traced those words over and over as I stood in front of the glass doors. I lowered my head and shuffled back across the parking lot under sun strong enough to blister my skin. The parking lot looked as isolated as I felt. I was married and a mother, but I was alone.

I closed my eyes as agony ripped across my chest. The very roof over my children's heads was one we couldn't afford. Nor could we afford the bills coming in and the ones past due. *How can we ever provide for them?*

I felt defeated. "I'm tired. So very tired," I cried out. "Tired of the circle, tired of the cycle." Darkness filled the spaces of my mind as I envisioned how my children's lives could be okay without me in it. As if on autopilot, I turned on the ignition; I no longer cared about waiting for the mortgage company staff to return. By muscle memory, the guidance of a higher power, or the laws of physics themselves, I made it back to my parents' house to pick up my kids.

Seeing their precious faces left me with one thought: *They deserve so much more than I will ever be able to give them.* I knew that was not how I should have been thinking, but I couldn't lift myself out of the mental fog. On the outside, I pulled it together enough to go through the daily routines for my children, yet on the inside, I was dying, I was lost, I was broke, and I was scared.

As we moved into foreclosure, we received a solicitation letter from a bankruptcy attorney that explained there might still be a way we could keep our home. The words *Chapter 13* brought a flicker of hope, as they suggested a new direction we could take to save our home *and* save us from the payday loan debt we were still so knee-deep in.

Gary Richard and I scraped together what little we had to pay for the attorney, and in 2005, we filed. I knew this was the way we had to go, yet it didn't stop the feeling of worthlessness or the fear of judgment from rising within. Our name would be in the paper, in black-and-white print, for all to see. Our failure put on public display for all to have their say. I wished I could have said, "I don't care what others think." But I cared. I cared a lot. I wanted to hide, but at least I no longer wanted to die.

After the bankruptcy, we tried to make better financial choices, but we had no discipline. We still spent money on things we wanted or things we wanted to do while we placed our utility bills on the back burner. I couldn't ask, "How did we get here?" I knew. We needed to budget, and we needed to stop living beyond our means. We needed to change, yet that was something we weren't willing to do.

So when the Chapter 13 bankruptcy payments began getting deducted from Gary Richard's paycheck, we went right back to that all-too-familiar place of falling income and rising financial need. This time, though, instead of rushing toward the crutch of a payday loan, I looked for other ways to supplement our income.

In my search to find alternate ways to earn more money, I came across a magazine article for a fertility clinic. The article said they were searching for egg donors and that donors could earn several thousand dollars. I had never heard of this kind of donation for money. I knew about plasma, as my husband had done that a few times over the years when we were low on cash. And from the movies, I had heard of sperm donors. But egg donors? As I continued to read the article, I felt as if the author was speaking right to me. The article spoke of the emotional pain that infertility brings to couples who desire to have a child and how donors help make their dream of having children come true. The donation could be a win-win for two families.

"I want to do this," I said to Gary Richard as I handed him the article. "This could really help us."

He read the article and then looked at me. "Are you sure?"

"Yes." When he nodded, I felt more at ease. "I will call tomorrow."

A week after my phone call, I went for an appointment to the fertility clinic that was two hours east of our home.

I walked through the glass doors of the doctors' offices and took the elevator to the second floor. I fiddled with an earring as I stared at the posters on the white walls of the waiting area. One showed two parents walking into beams of sunlight as they held the hands of their child. The other had a mother dressed in white who looked as if she was lying on a cloud, lifting her baby, who also wore white, high into the air.

"Caroline?" a woman in a white lab coat and black stilettos called out. I stood and approached her.

"Hi, I am Mary, a nurse and donor coordinator for the clinic," she said as she offered a hand for me to shake and smiled. She exposed bright white teeth outlined by dull red lipstick. "Follow me to my office."

We walked quietly down the hall to her office, and then she ushered me inside. Her eyes sparkled at me as she pointed at the chair.

Once we were both settled, she looked at me again and smiled. "Why are you interested in being a donor?"

Her voice was inviting, making me feel as if I could tell her anything. But I knew the truth—I needed to say whatever would be the "right answer." I thought about the flyers I read in the waiting room, which said: *Egg donation provides another family the gift of life.* That was the answer they wanted to hear. Not "I'm here only for the money."

So I returned her smile and began my speech. "I saw the article in the paper, and I already have had two healthy children," I told her. "So if I can do that for someone else, that would be rewarding for me."

Mary explained the screening process, which involved a medical exam, blood work, and psychological screening to ensure I understood the benefits and risks, as well as had the proper motivation to become a donor. Then once a recipient was matched to me, I would self-inject Lupron hormones to stop ovulation and then follicle-stimulating hormones to stimulate the growth of multiple follicles. After the eggs reached maturity, I would receive one final injection to prepare my ovaries to release the eggs. Then about two days later, I'd return here so they could retrieve them via a surgical procedure.

Shivers rolled down my spine at the thought of injecting myself with a medication that in the long term could harm my body. However, the $3,000 they were willing to pay convinced me it would be okay, because that was what my family needed. *Okay, I will do this just one time,* I told myself. *One time will be okay.*

A month after meeting with Mary, I completed the physical exam, had blood drawn, went in for ultrasounds, met with the counselor, and signed the consent forms that officially added me to the program. A week later I was matched with a recipient and began the injections of Lupron. That day I went to my bedroom and locked the door so the kids, who were playing in the other room, wouldn't come in. I sat the refrigerated vial on my nightstand and removed the orange-capped insulin syringe from the box of supplies Mary had given me. I lowered myself on the edge of my queen-size bed, allowing my legs to dangle over the side. I rubbed my upper thigh with the square pad saturated in alcohol, took a deep breath, pushed the tip of the needle through my pinched skin, and closed my eyes briefly. I pressed the plunger with my thumb and forced my eyes open so I could watch as the liquid disappeared from the syringe. Over the next few weeks, I performed my daily injections and went for a vaginal ultrasound to see how the follicles were growing.

"The sacs are large. They look really good," Mary said when I went in for my checkup. "I think we should be able to get at least twelve eggs. I will get you set up with outpatient surgery so we can do your retrieval. I'll call you later to tell you what time to check in at the hospital."

I nodded while looking at the paper map with arrows she slid in front of me.

"You will need a driver because you will be under anesthesia."

"Okay, I will have my husband take me," I said.

Two days later, I reported to the hospital with my sister-in-law, because Gary Richard was unable to get off work. I lay in the bed dressed in a thin white gown and surrounded by walls of curtains. The anesthesiologist came in and verified what they would give me to put me under. And a short while later, a nurse came and wheeled my bed down the long white hallway. There were faces in the room, and I watched as the anesthesiologist approached my arm, and then the next thing I knew, I woke back up in a place that looked like the room where I had started.

"How are you feeling?" my sister-in-law asked.

"I am good," I said sluggishly. "Is it all done?"

She nodded.

Mary entered the room. "You did great! Once you're feeling better, we'll do a follow up back in the office, where you will receive your compensation."

I nodded. I was tired and ready to go home. The rest of the evening I drifted in and out of sleep on the couch. My mom watched the kids until Gary Richard could pick them up when he got off work.

The kitchen door squeaked open, and feet softly brushed across the carpet, stopping in front of me.

"Mommy, are you okay?" Daniel asked as he touched my shoulder.

"I am okay, baby. I am just tired. Come, hug Mommy," I said, lifting my shoulder from the couch.

Ember, who had recently turned two, came around the corner and joined in the hug, and I kissed the tops of their heads, inhaling the bubble gum scent from the shampoo my mom used on their hair.

Gary Richard stood behind them. "Are you okay?"

"Yeah, will you just take care of them so I can sleep?"

"Of course. Are you hungry?"

I shook my head no and pulled my knees up to my chest along with the blanket.

I had intended for it to be only a one-time donation. However, after I recovered quickly and received the check, it turned into five times over the next year and a half. It became a transaction. I sold them a part of me, and they gave me what I needed. Once I received shots to keep me from having a baby, and now with every injection I pressed into my skin, this question arose within: *How did I get here again?*

CHAPTER 8

DRIVEWAY

"Why are they here?" My eyes widened as I turned to look at Gary Richard. We had just pulled out of our garage, heading out for an evening of family fun to celebrate the straight As Daniel had received on his fourth-grade report card.

He shrugged. "I don't know, but stay here with the kids while I go talk to them." He slammed the car door, then tucked the tips of his fingers in his jeans and walked down the gravel driveway toward the two sheriff deputies and their cars that were blocking the exit.

"Where's Dad going?" Daniel asked.

I fixed my eyes on the passenger window, trying to think of what I should say to Daniel, Ember, and Daniel's friend. I took a deep breath, hoping it would bring forth my sweet "mom voice," the one that automatically came out when I saw a newborn baby or talked to a puppy. Slapping a big smile on my face, I turned around. "Your dad will be right back, and then we can go have some fun." Daniel and his friend, who were both nine, nodded, then turned their eyes down to their handheld video games. Ember, who had just turned three, smiled as bright as her white shoes that dangled over her car seat.

After a few moments, Gary Richard returned to the car window and waved his fingers, signaling me to step outside. His eyes were wide, and his lips pressed so tightly together they looked frozen.

This isn't good. I could feel the nerves running through my trembling hand as I released my seat belt. Somehow I knew the words I had just spoken to the kids were no longer true.

After he walked far enough from the car that the kids couldn't overhear our conversation, Gary Richard turned to face me. "They need me to go downtown to the police station with them to ask me some questions."

"For what?" I tempered my words, trying to maintain my composure, since I knew the kids could see me.

"There were allegations made against me. They served me a restraining order. I don't have time to explain it now. They're waiting for me. I will explain it later, once I know more."

I wrapped my arms around my churning stomach and rapidly fired question after question. "What do I do? The kids are so excited to go. Do you think we can still go? What do I tell them? How long will you be gone?"

Gary Richard shook his head, pulled me into his chest for a quick goodbye hug, then turned and headed back to the end of the driveway.

I stood, frozen. On the outside, I couldn't feel my legs. On the inside, every part of me trembled. *What am I supposed to do now? Why is this happening again?* I pleaded with my mind to give up some answers, but there were none to give.

My eyes watered as I reflected on what I had seen from the driveway seven days ago on that perfect fall afternoon when all was as it should be. With one palm waving in the air and the other gripped around the steering wheel, I had driven down our road on my way back home from work, singing "My Life Is in Your Hands" along with gospel singer Kirk Franklin. I'd turned into our driveway, admiring how the blue sky complemented the burnt-orange and scarlet leaves that scattered across the ground. Streams from the October sun had danced through the gaps of the trees, and I'd stopped the car to capture what I was seeing—Gary Richard raking leaves into multicolored mini-mountains while Daniel and Ember leaped into them. Before my very eyes lay everything I had dreamed my family would be. Happy, laughing, safe in a home filled with love, surrounded by the white picket fence (although ours was chestnut). It was a fairy tale come true, not distorted by thoughts of struggle, poverty, adultery, lies, or crimes, but just a father with his children having a good time.

Now I stood in the same place in the driveway and watched a very different scene.

The crunch of gravel under the deputies' tires jolted me back to the present, and I knew I wasn't in the frame of mind to process anything going on with the kids being around because all I wanted to do was drop onto the ground, pull my legs into my chest, and wail.

I needed someone to help me process this nightmare. That would have to be my parents. But I couldn't take the kids with me, and I couldn't just drop them off unannounced at other people's homes. My mom raised me with the belief that it was impolite to invite myself over to someone's house. It was something, as a kid, she never allowed me to do, but in this situation, it was all I could do. I needed someone to keep the children for the evening so they could be safe and far away from anything that would make them feel confused or scared, and I was both.

I called a friend who lived close by to ask if Daniel and his friend could go there to play with her son. Then I called my coworker Regina, who had become like another grandmother to my children, and asked if she could keep Ember. I gave the same reason for the request both times: "I don't know what is going on, but the sheriffs just came to take him to the station."

I returned to the car, but this time I got in on the driver's side. I closed the door, took a deep breath, turned my head over my shoulder, and spoke to my son and his friend first.

"Hey, guys, I'm sorry, but we aren't able to go today."

Their mouths lowered, and they turned their eyes to each other as if to confirm that they both felt deflated.

"I promise we will still go. It will just have to be another day. But guess what?" I blurted out, hoping my pretend excitement would lighten the mood.

"What?" Daniel said.

"You get to go over to Ryan's house to play."

They gasped and bounced up and down on the seat.

I drove around the block and dropped off the boys, then before I pulled my car away from the curb, I turned my attention to Ember. It was easier to explain the change in plans to her. Such innocent unawareness on her face, and if her "go with the flow" eyes could have spoken, I think they would have said, *Okay, Mom, whatever you say.* She just needed to hear the name *Regina.*

"Guess who you get to go see? Regina!"

She grinned. She loved spending time with my friend.

After I dropped my daughter off, I went straight to my parents' house so I could vent, scream, talk it out, and try and wrap my head around what had just taken place. But every thought led back to only one clear, fair, honest question. I put it in the form of a prayer, but it was the first prayer I'd ever prayed with profanity laced between words. "What is going on, and why is it always something with him? Dear God, why is it always fucking something?" It was a question filled with emotional exhaustion, not just from the events of this day but from nine years leading up to this day.

For the last year, Gary Richard and I had been regularly attending the church we were married in. I'd been feeling as though something deep and significant was missing in our lives, and one Sunday after we didn't wake up until almost noon, I realized what it was.

"I think we should start taking the kids to church," I said to Gary Richard as I sat up in bed.

He looked at me oddly for a moment but then agreed. "Okay, why?"

"I want our family to be like those other families. The ones who get up early on Sunday, eat breakfast, and get dressed up. I think it looks neat."

He nodded and stretched his arms above his head.

"I also want the kids to learn about God. I feel like as parents we are supposed to take them at some point, aren't we?"

He yawned. "Okay, we can go."

Since we didn't know where else to attend and we had both liked the pastor who married us, we figured that was as good a church as any. A month after we started attending, Gary Richard began to help with the sound system, which was a perfect fit for his skills with technology and since he was still dabbling in disc jockey services. I helped in the nursery, which was a good fit for me, because Ember was right there alongside me, and Daniel was just down the hall in the children's church.

We attended a few church activities with other couples, including the pastor and his wife, who were in their sixties. We took our family photo for the church directory. It was a good photo too; it showed my perfect little family. A mom with shoulder-length blond hair with tones of wheat was resting her hands on the thighs of her little girl's red-cherry-patterned pants while nestling into the right arm of the dad. He smiled and showed off his stylish silver wire frames while wrapping his arms around his little boy, whose heart-shaped face matched the joy shining from his eyes. What more could I ask for? This was my beautiful family of four.

My family was all I needed, and tonight I couldn't hold or take care of any of them because I needed someone to take care of me.

"I don't understand," my mom said as she held me in her arms.

"I don't either." I shook my head as *Why is this happening? What is happening?* repeated over and over in my head.

Two hours later, my phone rang, jolting me out of the endless mental puzzle. I stared down at the name of the caller. *Unknown.* I exhaled heavily and answered.

"Caroline," Gary Richard said.

I closed my eyes, ready to be soothed by the calmness of his voice that had always felt like warm honey coating everything that ached—only this time it didn't.

"A teenage girl made an accusation that I inappropriately touched her. They're questioning me, and I don't know how much longer I'll be here."

"What?" I couldn't believe what he was telling me now. Someone else accusing him of inappropriate touching. I wanted to scream.

"I've got to go," he said. "Can you call my buddy's friend who is an attorney and ask him what I should do?"

I sighed. Being angry wasn't going to change this new situation we were in. "Yes" was all I could say. I hung up the phone before he could say anything else. I wanted to ask, "Did you do it?" But I couldn't. I knew someone could be listening to him, and I didn't want them to hear his answer. The answer I feared hearing most.

The walls of my parents' kitchen were closing in on me, so I staggered out to the front porch, where I called the attorney.

"You have reached the voicemail of—"

I hung up the phone and sat on the white wicker rocking chair. I rubbed my head in frustration and felt that now all-too-familiar ache in my stomach appear. The questions came again to my mind. *Why do things keep coming up with him? Why is he always the one accused?*

I left my parents' house and went home, where I called Regina and Ryan's mom, who both suggested I just let the kids spend the night and they would bring them home later the next day. I was relieved that I didn't have to find the energy to usher them to bed or fake a smile or field questions that I flat-out didn't have answers to, like when their dad would be coming home. I lay in the bed we shared and reached my arm over to feel the coolness of the empty sheets. I missed him.

I tossed and turned throughout the night, wondering what could be taking so long. Telling the darkness that filled my room, "He couldn't have done it. He *wouldn't* have done that . . . would he?" I received only the echoes of silence.

Twenty-four hours later, Gary Richard called and said they had released him from questioning and he was ready for me to pick him up. I made arrangements with Regina and Ryan's mom to drop the kids off at my parents', then I made the familiar drive to the station.

"Did you do it?" I fired at Gary Richard as soon as we pulled away from the police station. He was driving, as usual.

He scanned my face. "How could you ask me that? Of course I didn't."

"Why would she say you touched her then? Why would her mom file a restraining order against you?"

He shook his head. "I don't know. Maybe she thinks I'm cute. You know how teenage girls can have crushes on older guys. Maybe when I deejayed at the high school dance a few weeks ago, she started to like me and made up a story about us to look cool. Then told her friends, and her mom heard about it and called the cops. I don't know."

I pressed my cheek against the passenger-side window and watched the streetlights race by. His explanation didn't make sense, but yet it did. I remembered making up stories about boys I hadn't done things with to look cool in front of my teenage friends. My mind swirled as the window went dark, then light, then dark—exactly how my mind felt as I tried to process this information. I wanted to believe him, and when the window showed light, I did. But in the seconds it went dark, I found myself silently asking, *If you didn't do this, why do things keep coming up with you? Why are you always the one accused?*

Over the past nine years of our marriage, I had asked so many similar questions of myself. I asked with the belief that I would find clarity, that I would discover what was true.

I understood what he was saying about teenagers and older guys because as a teenager I had fallen for one myself—I had fallen for him. But this was different, and it still didn't answer the *whys* to all the questions I felt too confused and wrong to ask.

As we continued to drive home, I could feel the partially digested chicken sandwich I'd eaten for supper rise to my throat as if it were trying to reject the answer he just gave me, and I swallowed to push it away.

We didn't mention the incident again, and for the next few weeks, I was the supportive wife. That was a role I knew how to play because I had done it so many times. Trust his words, discount theirs, and prepare to fight against whatever these accusations may bring. As a wife, I believed this was what I had signed up for—to stand by his side for better or worse. And although nothing about this situation made sense, I found comfort playing this role and accepting the words he spoke to explain it all away. Those words validated my decision to stay in the marriage, and let me continue to hope that the images seared inside my mind of two sheriffs' cars blocking our drive would one day soon be exchanged for the images of a father playing with his children in the backyard.

CHAPTER 9

INTUITION

"You sure you don't want to go?" I said to Gary Richard as he sat on the couch in his palm tree pajama pants. "My family will wonder where you are."

"Yes, I'm sure. I don't feel like being around anyone right now," he said.

"Okay." I sighed in frustration. "Can we at least take a picture so that we can have a family photo on Thanksgiving?"

It was his turn to sigh now. "I'll take one of you and the kids."

In contrast to the hustle and bustle of the holiday season, the allegations against him had entered a period of silence. We didn't hear anything regarding the investigation as we moved through November, which I felt was a good indication that nothing further would take place. I knew the stress from it all was a lot to endure—after all, I felt tired and drained too—but I didn't understand why it made him feel like not being around anyone. He loved being around people. I saw it in the way his eyes lit up every time he entered a room and strutted across the floor to share exciting stories about riding Jet Skis or fires he had fought on the fire department he volunteered to join after Ember was born. But for whatever reason, he decided not to participate with my family, and I didn't ask why. Maybe because I was tired and just didn't want to deal with it. So instead I rolled my eyes, then corralled the kids inside my arms and smiled for the photo before heading to my aunt's house for Thanksgiving dinner.

Though everyone asked where Gary Richard was, and I made some lame excuse for his absence, we all enjoyed the day together. But I couldn't keep my mind from drifting back to Gary Richard and what was bothering him.

In the middle of the meal, my phone rang. I was surprised to see Gary Richard's number pop up. *Maybe he changed his mind and is coming over.*

"Hey, the Best Buy ad has a great price on a computer." Gary Richard's voice sounded as heavy as the plate filled with mashed potatoes and homemade noodles that I pushed forward on the table.

"Ooookay." I stood from the table to go outside to talk with him in private. *He can go to Best Buy, but not come here?*

"I think we should get this one for Daniel, because I don't think we will find another one for under two hundred dollars. If I go out there tonight, around six, I should be one of the first people in line when they open their doors in the morning."

I closed my eyes and shook my head toward the phone. How had he gone from moping around the house in his pajamas a few hours ago to this burst of excitement about shopping for a gift we had only briefly discussed a few days earlier?

"I thought you didn't feel like being around anyone," I said. "You didn't want to come with me, and now you want to go out to Best Buy."

"I told you I just don't feel like being around anyone. I don't want to sit around and visit."

An uneasy feeling fluttered in my stomach, but I didn't want to engage in an argument. It wasn't worth the fallout to me—especially not on a holiday in front of all my family. "Okay, if you want to go buy it, then go ahead," I told him, resigned to the fact that he was going to do it anyway. "Do you want me to bring you a plate home?"

"No."

I hung up, then pushed the phone into the pocket of my jeans as I returned to the table. No one seemed to notice I'd been missing—the family was laughing, eating, and continuing their lively conversation. I looked down at my plate of delicious homemade food, but I no longer had an appetite. Worry set in. Something was wrong with Gary Richard, but what?

The kids and I drove home to an empty house, and the solitude I felt reminded me that this day had strayed far from being a joyous family celebration of gratitude. I was over it. Nothing about Gary Richard's actions made sense, and his absence at my aunt's and now at home was so different from the tradition of holiday togetherness I had assumed it would be.

Shortly after nine, while I tucked Daniel into his bed, I thought of Gary Richard again, now certainly at Best Buy.

Is he cold? Does he regret his choice to camp out at the store? Did he take a blanket with him to bundle up? I closed my eyes to regain my focus.

Daniel looked up at me expectantly.

"You ready?" I said and smiled at him. "Let's say our prayers. Now I lay me down to sleep ..."

"I pray the Lord my soul to keep," Daniel added.

"My angels guide me through the night," I continued.

"Until I wake in the morning's light," Daniel whispered as I pressed my lips into his hair and then removed the glasses from his face.

I walked to the doorway and paused. "Goodnight, baby. I love you," I said and turned off the light.

"I love you too."

I thought about the prayer we'd just prayed. My mom taught it to me, and saying it together became a tradition, along with a goodnight kiss and the words *I love you* whispered before she turned off my light and left my room. I was glad I'd been able to continue that tradition with my children. At least that part of my life hadn't changed.

I walked into the living room, where I spotted Ember fast asleep on the couch and scooped her into my arms. I inhaled the watermelon scent of her hair as I lowered her onto her bed, then pressed my lips into her squishy cheek.

"Goodnight, baby. I love you." I pulled the cover to her shoulders and brushed the hair from her face.

I returned to the living room, plopped onto the couch, and flipped on the television. Though I was tired, I wasn't ready to go to bed yet—even though I knew I had to get up early in the morning to go shopping with my mom and sister. I stretched my legs down the couch, settled in, and watched the images flash on the television screen. I couldn't focus, though. Something was nagging at me deep in my gut. Something about how Gary Richard was acting.

I sat up and turned to stare at the computer. Doubt crept into my mind. *What is Gary Richard really up to?* I was determined to find out the truth. I headed to the computer and typed *Myspace* in the web browser. I didn't know what I was looking for, but based on the calm feeling that had now

replaced my uneasiness, I sensed this was where I was supposed to be.

Myspace was the social networking site that Gary Richard used for his disc jockey service and where he and I
jointly shared an account where we posted photos of our life
together. I had been on our page plenty of times, but since his
business page was always one he maintained separately, I'd
never had any reason to access it. Until tonight.

After a few unsuccessful password attempts, somehow I
finally guessed the correct password and got in. Immediately I
went to the area that contained messages, and within seconds,
I learned that my intuition had been correct to guide me here.
A storm of emotion took over every inch of my body as my
eyes traced photos of women in their forties to girls in their
teens. I read words he wrote that told them how sexy they
were, of plans to take trips together, and how he wished he
were spending his time with them instead of me. Each word
crashed into the shoreline of my marriage, exposing a reality I
hadn't seen. Or rather, I had seen but hadn't wanted to admit.

How could I have been so blind? How could I not have known?
A part of me wished I could unsee it, but the way my body
was trembling was a reminder I couldn't.

My legs bounced uncontrollably at the sight of his
betrayal and the silent replay of all the lies he had spoken
throughout the years.

"Caroline, you are the only one I want to be with."

"Caroline, I wouldn't cheat on you."

"Caroline, I won't hurt you again."

Tears cut down my cheeks and spotted my navy pajama
pants. I cried out, wanting to ease the pain and hoping the
fans in the children's rooms would mask the sound. I cried

not only for me but for everyone who had been impacted by his actions and my failure to respond to them. I cried because I no longer believed he didn't do what he had been accused of with the teenage girl. I cried for my kids, knowing their lives would forever be changed. I cried for fear of change, knowing I no longer had a choice. I could no longer deny and shake things off. I could no longer believe or pretend that my husband was who I wanted him to be.

One letter at a time, the truth of my marriage was unveiled, and I could no longer be the wife I had dreamed of being since childhood. I could no longer trust his words. And as each tear added weight to the damaged walls I had built over the years to protect our marriage, I knew our relationship didn't have the strength to sustain itself.

I stared at the images on the screen until they became blurry, mourning the death of the future I once saw so clearly. I wept for the fairy-tale ending I'd imagined, one I could no longer pretend would come true. I grieved for our family home, which, along with my heart, was broken. I cried for the loss of structure, validation, and the identity my marriage had given me for the last nine years. I ached for my children—that they didn't get the kind of father I dreamed they would have or that they deserved.

My heart seared with the pain of letting go, and I wrestled with the thought of wanting to cling to the familiar because it felt safer than facing the fear of moving into the unknown. I wanted to be angry and disgusted, but despair was the only thing I felt, and I wasn't sure how much more I could bear.

I couldn't control how bad I was shaking; I thought I might fall off the chair. And my breath was so shallow I felt as though I couldn't breathe. Just when I thought I might pass out, something warm cascaded over and around my body. And in that moment, I knew God was right there.

Like a weighted blanket, the pressure of the Divine touch was safe, and it wrapped around my pain. The crying stopped, and in the silence, I heard direction.

You can go. I have you.

The words brought a peace I hadn't felt before. They released the worry, and I no longer needed to question if the kids and I would be okay, because I knew we would. Then, as if someone had replaced my eyes, the blurry screen became crystal clear, and I didn't feel confused or afraid. I felt powerful, safe, and I was no longer willing to accept Gary Richard's mistreatment or sit idle or stay quiet or sacrifice my life for the title of *his wife*.

I didn't analyze what this clarity was, because instinctively I knew. And I no longer believed God only sat behind the vast blue curtain high above the ground. The Presence was with me, concerned about me and our situation. My shoulders straightened. I was ready to take the next step. It was time for Gary Richard to leave.

CHAPTER 10

EXIT PLAN

My heart raced as the darkness started to pull from the sky. I knew it was time to remove Gary Richard from our home, time for the exit plan to begin. I wasn't exactly sure what that plan was, but I had to figure it out as I sat in deafening silence for several hours, unable to sleep.

I figured he would be home around seven in the morning, carrying in the computer he purchased from Best Buy. I glanced at the clock. It was nearly that time. Since I didn't want him to know anything about what I'd found until I confronted him, I knew I needed to print off the proof before he got home. I put the incriminating papers in an envelope and tucked them in the back of the cabinet above the refrigerator. Well aware that we would someday soon be in divorce court, I wanted the communications between him and the girls to prove why I should have custody of our children. Protecting them was at the front of my mind, and the papers shielded me from his ability to spin the accusations around to make me seem unfit or crazy.

With the children still nestled into their beds and sleeping soundly, I made myself a cup of coffee, sat at the kitchen table, and waited for him to come home. As I waited, my mind went through every scenario I could come up with for how to confront him without the kids seeing anything that would damage them.

I climbed on the counter and pulled out the papers I had just hidden. For what seemed like the millionth time, I traced every word he wrote as if trying to sear them into my memory. The chains of the garage door clanged as they opened, grabbing my attention. Quickly, I shoved the papers back into the cabinet and hopped down, glanced at the numbers on the microwave, and saw them announce 7:30 a.m. Gary Richard was home.

I really wanted to confront him right away. But I feared that might wake up the kids—something I wanted to avoid. They didn't need to hear the accusations and excuses. But also my mom and sister were set to pick me up in a half hour to go shopping—something I had lost interest in.

Sure enough, he stepped into the kitchen, his arms carrying a large box. He looked tired but excited and smiled brightly at me.

"Hey," I said, feeling repulsed at seeing him and knowing how much he'd lied to me. I needed to keep my voice steady and not show my anger. "Did you have any trouble getting the computer?"

"Nope," he said, his voice sounding energetic. "I was right at the front of the line and was the second person to grab the voucher to take to the register."

I walked toward the coffee pot, wondering how his voice sounded so different from yesterday, as though whatever was bothering him had gone away. "That's awesome. Daniel is going to be excited."

"I know, I can't wait to see his face on Christmas morning. I'm so happy I went out there to get it."

I rolled my eyes and filled my cup as Gary Richard went into our bedroom to hide the computer in our closet.

"I'm going to take a shower, then try to sleep a little before the kids wake up," Gary Richard said as he popped back into the kitchen.

"Okay, I'll be gone before you get out. Mom is picking me up at eight."

He smiled and nodded, happy and unaware of what was soon coming his way.

By eight, Mom, Blair, and I headed out to find some Black Friday bargains. At each store, the other shoppers raced by me as I moved slowly down each aisle, not caring to be in the store, around people, or getting a bargain. All I could picture was Gary Richard at the computer, seducing all those women and those girls.

As the afternoon approached, we broke away from shopping to have lunch. I wasn't hungry, so I did more picking than actual eating.

"Are you feeling okay?" my mom asked.

I cringed inside. I'd never been able to hide my feelings from my mom. But I just wasn't ready to share this new information I'd discovered about Gary Richard. I offered a weak smile. "Yeah, why?"

"You haven't eaten very much, and you've been very quiet today."

I looked down at my plate. It looked the same as when the server brought it out. I lifted my eyes as heat brushed across my cheeks. "I'm just tired. I didn't sleep well last night.

My stomach was bothering me. I think I overate yesterday at Aunt Sally's."

Mom smiled and let out a small sigh. "The chocolate pies always mess with my stomach."

I wanted to tell her and my sister. I wanted to shout out, "No, I am not feeling okay. Let me tell you what I saw last night. Would *you* be feeling okay?" But I didn't want to explain it. Not yet. Not today. I needed to conserve my energy so I could think about the next step in my plan to get him out of the house.

At lunch, as Mom and Blair chatted about the deals they'd found and what else they wanted to purchase, my mind strategized. I decided it would be best to wait until Monday when Daniel was back at school. That meant I had to act as if everything was fine for the next three days. But I would force myself to do that, since Daniel was my first priority. I didn't want any confrontation in front of him—he was nine, and it wasn't anything I felt a child his age should see. I didn't know what Gary Richard's reaction would be. I anticipated he would deny everything and refuse to leave, so to combat the resistance, I needed to get him out strategically.

Throughout the weekend, I did my best to pretend nothing in my marriage had changed. Usually, weekends went by way too fast, but this one seemed as though it would never come to an end. I cooked meals. I cleaned the house while Gary Richard tinkered in the garage. I felt his breath creep like vines across my neck while lying next to him in bed. And with every moment, I prayed that somehow God would give me the strength for this next step.

The Monday morning sun streamed across my bed, inviting me into the day I had been waiting for. With eagerness, I jumped from my bed, ready to seize it. As I stepped into the bathroom Gary Richard and I shared, his woodsy cologne filled the air, reminding me of what was at stake. I wasn't going to give in this time. No matter what he tried to say or do.

"Have a great day at work!" I said to Gary Richard as he headed out the door.

He nodded, and as soon as the door closed behind him, I started the countdown. There was no going back.

I got Daniel up and fed, then Ember and I dropped him off at school. Back home, I ushered her into her room, where she began playing with her toys, and I started ripping his clothing from the hangers and stuffing them into yellow trash bags. I remembered the last time I'd packed clothes in garbage bags. That was when I was going to take Daniel and leave. But not this time. We were staying; Gary Richard was going. I dragged the bags into the garage and heaped them in the back of the SUV. I buckled Ember in her car seat, then backed out, gripping the steering wheel with determination.

I drove to Gary Richard's work, pulled in next to his car, which was sitting in front of his office window, and dialed his cell.

"Do you want your clothes in your car or outside on the sidewalk next to it?" I shouted into the phone, stepping between my car and Gary Richard's.

"Ummm, what?" Gary Richard's voice sounded bewildered.

"Do you want your clothing in your car or outside on the sidewalk next to your car?" I repeated matter-of-factly.

"Caroline, what are you talking about?"

"I am outside your office door in the parking lot. I have your clothes in my car, and I asked where you want them, because you are never coming back into our house ever again. I saw everything on your Myspace page. *Everything*. You are a liar, and I don't believe any words you say. We're getting a divorce. I'm done with you."

Silence.

Within moments, Gary Richard bolted out the door and raced toward me.

"Can we talk about this?" he said, his face looking flushed.

"No!" I declared and started walking toward the back of the car to unload his belongings.

Gary Richard propped his body against the door of my car to stop me from unloading it. "Caroline, please don't do this here, not at my work. If you want me to leave, I will go. But please take my things home. When I get off, I will pack them and leave. Please, please, wait until I get off."

I was so angry; I didn't care that his coworkers would see our scene. But I also knew his pleading wouldn't end until I gave in to what he wanted. I figured the only way to get him to go back inside was to tell him what he wanted to hear. "Okay, fine. I'll wait, but you are leaving."

"Okay, I will." His whole body seemed to relax a bit more. "Thank you, Caroline. I'll get everything when I get home. I promise." He walked toward the car door closest to Ember and opened it. "Hey, sweetie, look what Daddy has for you." He reached inside his pocket and pulled out three pieces of candy.

Ember's eyes lit up and she smiled, hugged and kissed him, then placed the candy in her lap.

"Thank you," he said again and headed back inside.

I slowly pulled out of the parking lot, making sure he didn't come back outside. Then I circled the building, pulled in next to his car, and piled his clothes on the pavement next to it. I hopped back into my SUV as clouds began releasing rain. Pulling out of the parking lot, I called him again. "Your clothes are outside next to your car. You may want to get them soon, because it is starting to rain."

Profanity slurred from his tongue as the derogatory names he called me seemed to run together. "I can't believe you are doing this to me!"

"I told you, you aren't coming back home." I threw the phone in the passenger seat, feeling the intoxication of finally being the one in control.

There was no turning back, no more believing the lies he spoke, no more disrespecting myself by setting boundaries and then allowing them to be broken—or not setting them at all. Enough was enough, and I was pressing forward audaciously.

A few hours later, Ember and I picked up Daniel from school. Without missing a beat in our routine, I had supper ready around six, and the three of us gathered around the kitchen table to eat. I knew I needed to address their father's absence, particularly to Daniel since he was older. "Hey, sweetie, Daddy won't be home for a little while, since he has to go out of town for work." I hated lying to my son, but how could I explain to a young child the real reasons for his father's abrupt departure? I simply didn't know how to explain to him that his dad would never be coming home again.

Daniel's head tilted slightly. And other than the soft groan, he seemed unfazed by what I had said.

Later that evening, my phone rang. I stared at Gary Richard's name as it came across my screen, debating if I had the energy to entertain whatever he had to say.

I sighed and, against my better judgment, answered.

"Hey, can I tell the kids goodnight?"

I sighed louder. "You can tell them goodnight, but that's it. I told them you are out of town for work."

"Okay." He sounded perturbed. "But, Caroline, I do think we need to talk."

"Don't even start."

After a few days, Gary Richard called again. "I think you should consider letting me come back home. You know we can't afford for me to keep spending money on hotel rooms."

He was right; we didn't have the money. I had been checking the account online and knew we had only a few hundred dollars, but I didn't see any transactions from hotels.

"Where did you stay last night?" I asked.

His voice caught with emotion. "In the parking lot of the rest area in between the semis."

My heart sank. I didn't want to feel sorry for him, but I did. The thought of him sleeping in his car tucked in the middle of trucks towering over him in the biting November air tugged at me.

I swallowed hard, determined to use a firm tone to make it clear that I was still in control. "Okay, I will let you stay here, but only until we get our tax money when we file in January. Then you can have the money and use that to get a place to stay. Also, there will be rules, and if you don't follow them, you are out of here."

"Okay, I will, I promise." He sounded relieved, grateful.

"We will not share a bed, nor will we have any intimate contact. We will not discuss working on our marriage, because we are getting divorced. Also, there will be no crying or arguing in front of the kids."

He stated that he understood my rules, and we agreed that roughly seventy-two hours after I had kicked him out, I would be allowing him back in. I couldn't believe it.

As I waited for him to return home, I wondered, *How did the strength I had in one moment feel like weakness in the next?*

God had given me such peace, direction, confidence, and strength to establish the exit plan and remove the danger from my home. Yet as I walked toward the couch, cradling the blankets to set up the area where he would be sleeping, I didn't feel peaceful, confident, or strong at all. I was scared, and financially, this seemed like the safer plan for us. Or maybe I was allowing him to return home out of a desire for comfort. The question gnawed at me: *Am I following God's exit plan or rewriting my own?*

CHAPTER 11

NEEDED

"Caroline, can you come to the church and pick up the children?" Pastor Bob asked. "Gary Richard is going to go to the hospital."

"Okay," I responded hesitantly, feeling confused. "I didn't realize they were there."

"Gary Richard came to talk with me and brought the kids. He told me you were at work tonight. He is having a hard time dealing with everything taking place in his life right now and feels like he needs to get help to get his mind in a better place."

I was stunned and remained silent as I tried to wrap my mind around Pastor Bob's words. I had just left the house a few hours before to work on some reports for my boss at the hospital. Gary Richard seemed fine when I left.

"I'm going to take Gary Richard out there, but I don't want the kids to get worried. Can you come to get them before we go?"

"Yes, I'm on my way."

I rushed out of the office and flew down the highway, trying to unscramble what was happening. Gary Richard had been back home for only a week, and this emotional breakdown felt like a complete violation of my rules. Anger began seething within.

Pastor Bob greeted me at the door, then ushered me down the hallway, where I saw the top of Gary Richard's white hat. I felt irritated by his presence as he leaned in the doorway of the children's room with his head hanging down.

Ignoring him, I drew my focus toward the kids. "Hey, what are you two doing?" I asked and smiled.

They rushed to me, nearly knocking me off balance as they wrapped their arms around my legs and waist.

"Daddy is going to go with Pastor Bob for a little while. Hug him, and then we will go home."

Pastor Bob interrupted my thoughts as we headed toward the entryway. "May I pray for your family?"

Without looking at Gary Richard, I simply nodded.

We formed a circle. I clutched Pastor Bob's hand in my left and Ember's in my right. We bowed our heads, and I closed my eyes.

"Heavenly Father, I raise this family to you," Pastor Bob's words began. "Strengthen their marriage ..."

My eyes jolted open and furiously began tracing the floor. I wasn't praying for my marriage. No way was I doing that. I already knew what God wanted for our marriage, I knew the day I sat at the computer, and I wasn't asking God to do anything to save it. I understood why Pastor Bob would want our marriage to last; he was the one who gave us the vows to say nine years ago. I also knew by the hope he had that he believed his prayer could bring repair, and I knew that meant Gary Richard hadn't told him the whole story.

The kids and I made our way home. I was relieved they didn't seem impacted by what had happened or ask questions that I didn't have the energy to create an answer for. A few hours later, I put them into their beds, and while I was straightening up the house, I heard the beep of my phone, indicating I had a text message. I grabbed it from the couch.

They are admitting me, but the floor is full. So they are sending me to the hospital down south.

My eyes glanced over the words and the selfie Gary Richard had sent. From the monitors and machines mounted to the walls behind him, I could tell he was still in the emergency room. And his puckered bottom lip clearly indicated he wanted my sympathy.

Not this time, buddy, I thought as I tossed the phone on the cushions and rolled my eyes. Though I walked away without responding, I felt relieved that he had another place to stay.

Over the next few days, I stayed busy by keeping up a routine for the kids and myself—chores, meals, bedtime, and baths. I remained in a pattern with my emotions too. No tears, no empathy. I was hardened. Hardened to protect myself from losing it and hardened to protect my kids from seeing it if I did. Hardened when Gary Richard called to give updates on how much longer he anticipated being at the hospital. Hardened to his relentless cries into the phone, saying he wanted to work on our relationship and begging for another chance. Hardened because I wanted to be cruel.

When a social worker called after Gary Richard had been in the hospital for four days, and asked if I could come to the hospital to have a "family meeting," I clenched my fist, ready to shout no, but then sighed. I could be hardened toward him—but not toward the social worker. I was sure she didn't know the full story either. "Yes, I'll come." Even though it was against my better judgment.

The next day, I walked down the white hallway toward the two ladies sitting at the desk behind a sliding glass window and announced that I was there for a meeting.

"Name?" she asked.

I leaned in and lowered my voice. "Caroline Downey." Then I craned my neck to look down the empty hallway to confirm nobody heard me checking in for behavioral health services.

The door buzzed. "Turn left at the hallway, and the conference room is at the end."

Inside the conference room, I saw a man and two women sitting at a large table with Gary Richard across from them. One of the women introduced herself as the social worker who had called me. She thanked me for coming, then gestured for me to take the empty seat next to Gary Richard.

I gave him a brief, weak smile. He smiled back.

"We called this meeting to have an open discussion regarding Gary Richard's treatment plan as he transitions out of here," she said, then pointed toward the woman sitting next to her. "This is Gary Richard's nurse." Then she nodded toward the man. "And this is his doctor."

I nodded my acknowledgment to each of them and then turned my attention back to her.

She peered at Gary Richard as though they had rehearsed this exchange. "Is there anything you would like to say to Caroline?"

Gary Richard looked down at the table, then up at me with the same puckered lips he had in the photo. "Thank you for coming. As part of my plan, they need to know where I will be staying. Am I able to stay at the house with you and the kids?"

I swallowed hard, feeling as though I was being manipulated. Heat crept across my cheeks at the thought of having to respond publicly. I wanted to shout, "No! He isn't my problem to deal with anymore. I want to be divorced from him." But I could feel the expectation in their stares—stares that felt like spotlights shining on my face. I knew he didn't have anywhere else to go. His grandmother passed away three weeks after Ember was born, and his dad's home was neither safe nor stable due to his alcohol addiction.

"Yes," I whispered.

"Thank you," Gary Richard said as his eyes flashed past my face toward the door.

I turned my head and saw two women giddily peeking inside. They quickly shuffled away from the door as the nurse said, "Ladies, go back to your rooms, please."

I looked inquisitively at Gary Richard. He shrugged and smirked.

"Gary Richard," the social worker continued, "would you like to tell Caroline what you told us about what you feel caused you to reach out to women on the internet?"

His unsettled eyes glanced around. "I needed attention. I felt like you didn't love me because you didn't pay attention to me, not like you used to. I need to feel loved. I need your attention. When I ask you to sit down with me so we can watch TV and spend time together, you don't because you're either busy vacuuming or taking care of the kids. You're always running around the house in sweats and oversized T-shirts; you don't dress up for me like you used to. They showed me attention, and I just got caught up in talking to them."

I narrowed my eyes as my thoughts frantically raced. He wasn't wrong about my lack of attention, my desire to take care of our home and kids, or my comfort wearing those clothes. But was he really trying to blame me for his actions? Were they? Did he tell them everything I saw?

"None of those things are excuses for what I have done to you, and I am sorry, but it is nice to feel needed." He blinked back tears.

I didn't respond.

After a moment's awkward silence between us, the social worker began again. "He told us about the arrangement you had at home regarding not sharing a bed and about not wanting to discuss working on your marriage. Are those still the boundaries you would like him to follow when he comes home?"

I nodded. "And not talking or being emotional in front of our children."

"I won't," Gary Richard declared.

The social worker asked where I was parked and told me if I wanted to pull the car around, they would wrap up the paperwork they needed to release him. We exchanged handshakes and goodbyes, then I made my way back down the long white hallway and heard the echoes of the metal doors jolting open.

"Mrs. Downey!" a woman shouted.

I pivoted and saw the nurse approaching me.

"I shouldn't be doing this, but I can't let you leave here and not tell you this. If you were considering going back to him, don't. I hear him call you, then watch as he hangs up and calls another woman who isn't you. I have watched him flirt with our staff and the other patients. I used to be married to a man just like him. They are very manipulative. I took him back, and I wish someone would have told me not to. That is why I have to say this to you." Her face looked as genuine as her words felt, and because I too worked in healthcare, I knew the risk she was taking.

"Thank you for telling me that. I am not taking him back. I have no desire to. I just want to be divorced."

With a slight smile, she squeezed my shoulder and nodded.

I pulled the car under the canopy that stretched over the sidewalk and waited for Gary Richard to come outside. I replayed the nurse's words over and over in my mind. Each time, her voice sounded more and more like the voice of an angel. She had risked her job to protect me, a woman she didn't even know. Although I had no plans of staying with him, her words confirmed that I was on the right path with the plan to remove him from my home. The sound of Gary Richard opening the door pulled me back to the task at hand, which was to get home and temporarily coexist until he had the money in January to move out.

"Could you take me to get something to eat?" Gary Richard asked as soon as he got into the car.

I nodded, wondering how he could feel like eating after all this, and pulled into the Burger King drive-through.

A heavy silence settled over us as we drove home. I felt like a shell, sitting very much alone next to the man I once couldn't keep my hands from caressing as we flew down this same highway. Now everything about his presence irritated me, including the way he crumpled his sandwich wrapper. I could feel him staring at me, hoping I would look at him. I refused to give him the pleasure.

We pulled up to my parents' house, and Gary Richard stayed in the car while I went inside to get Ember. I held her hand as we walked toward the car, then stopped and pointed at the passenger window. Gary Richard threw open the door, her eyes widened like the moon, and his arms swallowed her body like light swallows the darkness from the sky.

She was excited to have her daddy home and told him about *Dora the Explorer* and the other shows she'd watched as we made our way to pick up Daniel from school.

"Hey, buddy," Gary Richard said as our son got in the car.

"Dad!" Daniel hurled his arms over the passenger seat and around Gary Richard's neck.

Gary Richard smiled, and so did I.

We made our way home, back into our routines of early mornings, work, school, and bedtimes, and moved further into December. Gary Richard knew the same rules still applied—no sharing a bed with me and no talking about our relationship. However, one night after the kids had gone to bed, he approached me as I sat in the living room.

"Caroline, can we talk about us, please?" his voice held a pleading tone.

"No, I already told you, I am not changing my mind. I am at peace with my decision. You need to find some for you and your life." I shrugged as I stood to leave the room.

His eyes lowered to the carpet.

The sight of his submission made me feel in control. A dangerous power pulsated throughout every part of my body. I felt like when I was sixteen, willing to surrender to whatever Gary Richard needed from me, but this time I was in the driver's seat. I pressed my fingertips into his shoulders and yanked his body forward until it pinned me to the wall while I pressed my lips firmly into his. I needed him, but not him. I needed the shell of him to escape from the anger, the stress, the desire, and the disgust. I needed to get lost inside his human touch.

The next morning the sunlight streaked across the lavender sheet draped over Gary Richard's bare hips.

"Good morning!" he said as he leaned back and placed his arms over his head.

My mouth was almost too dry to speak. I nodded and croaked out a quick "Morning."

"Last night was amazing! We haven't been together like that in years. That felt like how it did when I first met you."

I shifted uncomfortably to the edge of the bed, then walked toward the closet. I tried to determine if I felt offended, complimented, or ashamed that I had broken my boundaries and allowed him back into our bed. I wrapped a robe around me and turned back to face him. "This isn't happening again."

He smirked.

I knew he didn't believe me. I wasn't sure if I believed me either, but I knew if I wanted him to take my desire for a divorce seriously, we couldn't do that again. I couldn't put myself in a situation where I needed to rely on him like that. Over the next few days, I felt back on track, focused, unwilling to communicate with him except about things that pertained to the kids. So one afternoon, when I walked out of work and noticed I had a flat tire, I debated whether I should call my dad or Gary Richard for help.

I chose Gary Richard. "I have a flat tire. Do you think you can come help me? If not, I can call my dad."

"I will be right there," he said, sounding excited. "Where did you park?"

"I'm on the ramp in the parking garage that goes to the top level."

"Okay, on my way."

He made it there in about fifteen minutes and aired it up, and I was on my way. As I drove home, I thought how nice it was to be able to call him, and I appreciated how willing he was to help me. *Maybe we can get along when all this is over, at least for the kids.*

The next morning it started to get colder in the house, and I noticed the furnace wasn't clicking on. I called Gary Richard at work.

"Hey, was the furnace working when you left this morning?" I asked.

"I think so. Why?"

"Well, I don't know why, but it isn't turning on. Do you know what I need to do?"

"I can break away from here and come look at it. I'll be right there."

"Okay, are you sure your boss won't care if you leave?"

"No, he doesn't care. See you in a minute."

Gary Richard arrived and went down the stairs that led to the dirt-floor basement. I heard his feet almost immediately run back up the stairs. "Okay, try it now. I fixed it."

I went to the thermostat and could smell the warm musty air that was beginning to flow from the vent. I shook my head in surprise. "You fixed it fast. What was the matter with it?"

"Oh, the switch on the side of the furnace wasn't turned on."

"How could the switch get turned off?"

He shrugged. "I'm going to go back to work."

"Thank you."

He grinned and headed out the door.

Again, I felt the relief of being able to call him for help. Although I still planned for him to move out in January, it was sure nice having him around the house for situations like this. His help eased the burden of trying to maintain everything by myself.

It brought comfort again two days later as Daniel, Ember, and I loaded up the car to go to Daniel's weightlifting practice. As we approached the green light at the intersection, the car moaned, and the gas pedal fell powerlessly to the floor. "Oh, no no no no," I cried out. "Please no!"

The car was losing momentum, and I feared we would get hit from behind or the side. If we continued to slow at this rate, we'd soon be stalled right in the middle of the road.

My heart was racing. I looked at Daniel, who was looking at me with a terrified and confused expression. I fumbled to find the button to turn on the hazards. By God's grace, we rolled through the lane and onto the shoulder. I pressed my forehead into the steering wheel and instructed Daniel to grab my phone.

My hands trembled as I called Gary Richard. "We just broke down. We barely made it through the intersection." I started to sob.

"Caroline, it's okay. You are going to be okay. I will be right there; I am not far away."

His gentle manner and honeyed tone confirmed what he had said the day at the hospital—he needed to be needed.

And I needed him to come to my rescue again. I needed the protection I felt in his voice. I needed the safety I felt when he showed up with my dad to tow the car away. I needed the direction he gave when he told me I could borrow his car if I needed one. I needed the compassion I felt when he ran his knuckle down my cheek to wipe the tears away. I needed the peace I felt when he reassured me everything would be okay. And with that, my hardened heart began to melt once again.

CHAPTER 12

THIS LITTLE CLOWN

"Caroline, your niece isn't feeling well. Are you able to pick her up from school?" It was Nurse Sara at the elementary school where my son and nieces attended.

"Is she okay?"

"She has a stomach ache. I gave her a peppermint, and it still hasn't gotten better. I tried calling her parents, but neither of them answered."

"I'll be right there," I said.

I buckled Ember into the back seat of Gary Richard's car, since my dad was still trying to fix mine. Fortunately, this Monday, the eighteenth of December, I was off work, and Gary Richard had made arrangements to ride with one of his coworkers to the office so I could have the car to take Daniel to school and go to the grocery store.

Since the school was only a mile east of our house, I reached the parking lot in minutes. I held Ember's hand as I checked in at the secretary's desk and then made my way to Nurse Sara's office, which was across the hall. She greeted me at the doorway and opened her palm toward a line of chairs against the wall where my niece sat with her knees pulled to her chest and her face tucked between them.

I combed my fingers through her soft caramel hair. "Hi, beautiful. I hear you aren't feeling well. Are you ready to go? You can lie down at my house until your mom or dad get home."

Her head tilted back, and her feet slid to the floor.

"Go get your stuff from your classroom and then wait in the office. I will be right there," Sara instructed.

Ember grabbed my niece's hand, excited that she would be coming home with us.

"Can she walk with me?" my niece asked.

"Sure," I said. "Just come right back so you don't disrupt the class."

As my niece and daughter headed down the hallway, Sara and I chatted. She and I had known each other for years, as she had been Daniel's elementary school nurse, and she had also been my nurse at the obstetrics office when I was pregnant with Ember. Nothing about our small talk felt out of the ordinary until Sara said, "I hear you and your husband have some difficult things going on?"

I drew my brows together, wondering what she had heard. *Is she talking about the sheriffs in our driveway?* That would make sense, I knew, because we lived in a small section of town and people talked. *That has to be what she means. She couldn't know what I found on the computer, or about Gary Richard's recent hospital stay, could she? No.*

Feeling sure the incident with the sheriffs had to be what she was referring to, I nodded.

"I'm sorry that is happening to you. Marriage is tough when there's infidelity. It's so hard to regain that trust to be able to work things out."

My body tensed.

"Ms. Webster."

What in the world is she talking about? What does my son's previous teacher have to do with anything?

"I told her she should tell you."

My pulse began to race. "Tell me what?"

Sara, who just moments ago had been so chatty, now lost her tongue. Her eyes looked as if they were saying, *Let me take back the words I just said and move this conversation in another direction.*

I glared back at her in response: *There's no other way to go.*

"After you and your husband attended a parent-teacher conference," she said slowly, then drew a deep breath, "she came to me for advice, because she felt uncomfortable with your husband being at the table."

Warmth prickled across my skin as I watched Sara clutch her hands. "Why?"

"They . . . slept together the summer before Daniel was in her class . . . in the bathroom at a wedding reception he deejayed at for one of her friends."

A sudden cold hit my core, and tears filled my eyes.

Sara handed me a soft tissue from her desk. "I'm sorry," she whispered. She wrapped her arm across my back, pulling my face closer to hers. "I thought you already knew. When I heard you and your husband were having issues, I thought that was why."

My stomach dropped with the weight of disbelief, shock, and disgust all piled in like unwelcome guests. I didn't need to ask for confirmation; the details gave it. I still didn't know how she could have found out about our marital troubles, but at this point, I no longer cared.

My mind jolted back to the night of that reception. I remembered him coming home and not coming straight to bed. I remembered seeing the light from the television illuminate the wall as I walked toward the living room to check on him. I remembered him saying, "I'm not tired yet, so I'm going to watch TV for a while." I also remembered him saying, "Tonight I found out who Daniel's teacher will be next year." And I remembered smiling when he said her name because that was the teacher I prayed our son would get.

I dabbed the corners of my eyes. Although my marriage was over before I entered this office, the pain of being betrayed by a teacher I trusted and the embarrassment of knowing my family's dysfunction was a subject of discussion at my son's school stung and magnified the pain I already suffered from.

"Thank you for telling me," I uttered as a slow smile began to build, hoping it would alleviate the sadness I also saw in Sara's eyes.

I turned my attention to signing my niece out of school and escorting her and Ember back to the car. I buckled in Ember, then staggered around to the driver's side and gripped the steering wheel to head home, which now felt like hours away from the school.

The girls were quiet; my mind wasn't.

What is wrong with me that my husband cheats?

How stupid am I?

Does everyone know except me?

How could he be with her?

I am prettier than she is, right?

How does a married man sleep with his son's teacher?

How does a teacher sleep with her student's married father?

Back home we made our way toward the kitchen. My niece shuffled across the floor, holding her hands on top of her stomach.

Oh, honey, I thought. *I feel sick too.*

Over the next couple hours, I fixed Ember's lunch, tended to my niece's needs, and periodically sobbed behind the locked bathroom door. I greeted my sister-in-law with a smile when she arrived to pick up my niece. I spoke in an excited tone when I picked up Daniel from school and again when Gary Richard came home around six that evening. But I avoided interacting with him like the plague. So I stayed busy with housework while he stayed busy out in the garage.

Around nine, I kissed the kids goodnight and tucked each of them into their beds, then, with Gary Richard still distracted in the garage, I grabbed the phone to call my sister-in-law, Tabitha, to share what I had learned at school.

I pressed my mouth into the receiver so she could hear my whispers. "You know what the nurse told me today about Gary Richard when I picked up your daughter?" I continued with the details until she gasped.

"You've got to be kidding me!"

I vigorously shook my head into the phone. "Nope, they're gross. Who does that?"

I paced back and forth in front of the living room window, periodically looking into the kitchen to make sure Gary Richard wasn't coming in. "How can she look me in the eyes and smile at me knowing what she has done? How can *he*?"

"He's an idiot! I can't believe he would sleep with her. Are you going to confront him?"

I drew a deep breath. "Yes, I don't know when. You know he'll deny it. But it doesn't matter, because I already know it's true. Part of me wonders what's the point, since our marriage is already over. He makes me—" I heard him turn off the music in the garage. "Gotta go. I think he is coming inside."

I hurried to the kitchen and placed the phone on the stand just as Gary Richard entered.

"Who were you talking too?" he asked.

"Tabitha. I wanted to check in and see how my niece was feeling."

He cocked his head back. "Sure you weren't talking about what the nurse told you about me?"

I froze. It felt like he had clenched his fist inside my chest and throat.

"You weren't talking about the nurse telling you I slept with Daniel's teacher? How you think I'm gross?"

His smirk sent shivers down my spine. "How did you know what I said to her?"

"You think I would sleep with her? Please." He rolled his eyes. "She's lying to you."

I staggered backward as his eyes raked my body with contempt. "How did you hear my conversation?"

He edged closer. "You say you don't want to talk to me. You don't want to talk about working things out between us, but you have no problem talking *about* me."

He was now close enough that his breath burned my face. "How, how did you—"

"Don't worry about how I heard what you said. Tonight we are going to talk about us whether you like it or not. I am tired of doing things your way."

Like a rabid dog, Gary Richard bolted into the garage. I could hear him throwing around tools on his tool bench.

What is he—

He rushed into the kitchen and lunged at me, pushing his wrist in front of my face.

"If I can't have you, then I don't want to live." He raised the blade of the gray box cutter in the air. "You are going to watch me do this, because you're the reason I'm doing it." He pressed the tip of the blade firmly into the skin of his left wrist and swiped.

I pressed my eyes tight. I never knew you could hear skin being sliced. It sounded as though he sliced the skin of an apple. He sucked in air between his teeth as tears poured down my cheeks.

"Look at me!" he demanded. "Look at me!"

I cracked my eyes open, blinking back the water, trying to bring him into focus. But his face was blurry. The only thing I could make out was the outline of his thin silver-framed glasses and red flowing like lava from the crack on the wrist that he now held up in front of my face.

"Are you happy? Is this what you wanted?" He scoffed. "Of course it is. You don't want me. You don't want me here." He sliced his wrist again.

"Please, Gary Richard! Don't, please." His wrist followed every movement my head made, leaving me no choice but to run. I pushed against him to get him out of the way, then darted toward the living room and down the hall. I halted outside Daniel's door.

Where can I go? Where can I hide?

I couldn't risk going any closer. I couldn't risk waking up Daniel. I hoped the fans in both of the kids' rooms were loud enough to keep them safe in their slumber. Where their dreams were sweet and keeping them far away from this nightmare I couldn't escape.

I pivoted and ran forcefully into Gary Richard's chest. The corners of his mouth rose as he captured me in his arms.

"Where do you think you are going?" He backed me into the corner where the wall met the back of the wraparound couch. My knees buckled, and I slid down the paneled wall and into his control.

"Gary Richard, please don't do this. I love you."

He crouched down in front of me, letting the blade dangle between his legs. "You don't love me. You're a liar." Droplets of spit splashed my face. "If you loved me, you wouldn't treat me like this. Walking around here, giving me the cold shoulder, acting like you're so much better than me. I am sick of you, and I am sick of this." He raised the blade.

I buried my head in my hands. I could feel the warm metal press against my forearm as he wrapped his hands around both of my arms.

"Get up. I told you, you're going to watch."

"I don't want to. Please stop!" I pleaded.

"Get up and go in the kitchen right now."

I staggered to my feet, using the back of the couch for support. I dragged myself toward the kitchen as Gary Richard's breath scorched the back of my neck like a blow-dryer held too close to the skin.

"Sit down!" he commanded.

I sat, silent and afraid, which seemed to give him a green light for his rage. He kept insisting we were going to talk, yet all I kept hearing him say was that I wasn't a good wife because I never gave him attention, I was stupid because I believed everything I heard, I never cared about him. Then he would horizontally slice one of his wrists again, alternating between his left and right. His blood ran as streams of water fell from my eyes and dripped onto my pants, making circles. Circles that formed over and over, just like the hands moved round and round on the clock, hour after hour of Gary Richard's words pushing me out of his love circle, then punishing me with every slice for no longer being in it.

When he wasn't cutting, he paced the length of the island counter that ran down the center of the kitchen, guarding the phones he had piled in the middle. When I mustered the courage to ask if he would let me go, he mimicked my crying and pleas.

How is this my life? How did I get here?

Here—where everything was unsafe and scary. Where nothing made sense except the terror of not knowing if either of us would survive his behavior.

As the hours rolled past midnight, he yawned, and I saw an opening.

"Gary Richard, it's after midnight, and we both have to go to work in the morning. Can we please just go to bed?" I begged.

"No. We aren't going to bed until I say we are going to bed."

"Can I go to the bathroom then? I need to go pee."

"You aren't going anywhere." My request fed his anger, and his voice grew louder. "I told you that!"

"Please, Gary Richard, I really need to go."

"Get up."

I used the table to push my body up from the bench and walked toward the doorway. Gary Richard barged in front of me and began nuzzling my face like a cat, scratching my forehead with his unshaved cheek.

"Why are you making me do this, Caroline? Why?" He pulled his wrist in front of my eyes. It now looked like minced meat—raw and bloody. "See what you made me do. See what I did for you. I love you." Then, as if applying blush to my face, he slid his wrist across my cheek.

My stomach turned with one whiff of the pungent metallic scent. I felt humiliated, all dignity tossed aside like a rag doll. I was his toy, his puppet on a string.

"You can go, but I'm coming into the bathroom with you."

I watched my feet brush the carpet that led into the bathroom. *Why didn't I hold it?* Over the years, I had urinated in front of him many times, because we had only one bathroom, so it had become a way to conserve time while he got ready for work or because I couldn't wait for him to finish his shower. Then it had been familiar, comfortable. Now, trembling to lower my pants, I felt violated. The same blue eyes that once filled me with comfort, passion, and desire now burned holes in me.

My face grew warm as Gary Richard perched himself in the corner, his presence sucking the ventilation from the room. I could feel the blood hardening on my cheek, and as I moved toward the sink to wash my hands, I raised my eyes to the mirror. I saw Gary Richard's angry reflection towering over mine. I wanted to wash the blood away from my face, but I couldn't ask, nor was I brave enough to do it without asking. It was his mark, his territory claimed. To wipe it away would bring even more rage. I turned and walked back toward the kitchen with strokes of dark maroon across my cheeks, the obedient clown in his circus.

He marched behind me, then announced to the empty room, "I will die before I give you a divorce."

I shrugged, and he erupted as if I'd sprayed gasoline on his flame. He stomped toward a glass of water on the counter and chucked it into the air. I jumped back as a thousand shiny splinters crashed around my toes. I quickly closed my eyes to hide from whatever was coming next—a punch, a slash to my body—then I heard feet move in the distance and stop. Silence and the faint tick of the clock filled the room.

I peeked at the clock to see the time: 3:30 a.m. Muffled sobs now erupted from the base of the doorway. I opened my eyes more fully. Gary Richard's shoulders slumped over his knees, and his back jerked as he sniffled between choppy breaths. I looked around for someone to guide me on what I should do. *Do I run or call 911 or . . . ?* I buried my fingers into my scalp, trying to make sense of what was happening, trying to hold on to something that felt sane. I pulled air deep into my lungs and knelt beside Gary Richard.

"Hey, are you okay?" It was a dumb thing to ask, I knew, but I was at a loss for what else to say.

Water soaked his face and his lips trembled, out of control. "I'm sorry, Caroline, I am sorry. I didn't want to hurt you."

I pulled his head into my breast, as I would often do with my children when they were frightened or hurt. "I know, Gary Richard, I know."

"Will you hold me?" His voice sounded like a little child's. It broke my heart.

I sprawled my legs across the floor and nestled his upper body between them. For the next hour, I ran my left hand over his temple and through his hair as I rocked him back and forth. I traced the blood that felt like cement on his wrist as my mind went into a trance over everything that had just transpired.

He was sorry; he always was. That was the circular theme of our marriage over these last nine years. Maybe I really was a clown. Our marriage, my life, sure felt like a circus. I knew I was a joke to everyone at the school, a joke to every woman he had been with. For years I was his entertainment, idly standing by as he held my heart like a balloon and manipulated it into whatever shape he wanted it. He was right; I was stupid. I believed I was safe with him, yet as I stroked his arm, the joke was on me for not recognizing the face of an enemy. I closed my eyes and silently prayed. *Dear Lord, if you get me through this, I will go to the police station in the morning and remove this danger from our lives.*

I opened my eyes and whispered, "Gary Richard, let's move into our bed and get a little sleep. It's four thirty."

He wiped the tears from his face, grabbed my hand, and led me toward our bedroom.

I crawled in next to him, pulling the blanket up to my neck, exposing my wiggling toes, and quietly entertaining myself with the nursery rhyme my mom taught me as a child: *This little piggy went to the market, this little piggy stayed home . . .* I fixated my eyes on the slats of the blind and exaggerated my smile until I felt the blood on my cheek crack. I *was* a clown, ready to take the stage. And in a few hours, *this little clown* would be brave.

CHAPTER 13

BEHIND THE GLASS

Piece by piece, I placed the shards of glass in my hand. My body was exhausted from the terror that had ended only a few hours before, and because I didn't sleep at all. Now two hours later, as I picked up the pieces from all the damage done, I knew that after Gary Richard left for work in the next twenty minutes, the only direction I could move was to the police station.

Gary Richard walked into the kitchen, still damp from his shower, as if it were just another morning. He wore his warm citrusy cedarwood cologne, and his slicked black hair shone from the gel he had in it. He grabbed his ritual can of Dr Pepper, then picked up his car keys and wallet from the counter. He turned toward the table where I sat clutching a warm mug of coffee. "Are you working today?"

"Yes," I replied quickly and took a sip, hoping he didn't know what I had planned.

His eyes twinkled as he smiled, then headed out the door. And I wondered why he wore no signs on his face of what had happened and uttered no words about it. No trace of feeling somber, expressions of regret, or exhaustion in his eyelids. Although the cuffs of his button-down shirt covered his wrists, I wondered if they looked as refreshed as the rest of him.

Moments later, the sound of the garage door opening triggered me into action like a starter pistol at the beginning of a race. I sprinted into the living room and peered through the slats of the blind as Gary Richard's car turned from our driveway and onto the street. Reassured that he was gone, I ran back into the kitchen to call work to let them know I was going to be late.

"Is everything okay?" my friend Regina asked.

"Yes and no. I mean, it is okay, I'm okay, but I need to go to the police station before I come to work."

"What?" Her voice sounded like her hand was covering her mouth. "Wait, what? Why? What happened?"

"I will tell you when I get to work. I don't have time to talk about it now, but I promise I am okay. I just need to go to the police station and get a restraining order against Gary Richard." I hated making that announcement and then hanging up, but I needed to get her off the phone so I could call my brother.

"Okay. Will you keep me updated?"

"Yes, I'll call you when I leave the station." I hung up with Regina, then dialed my brother's house. Tabitha answered.

"Hey, something crazy happened last night with Gary Richard. Do you think—"

"What happened?"

"He wouldn't let me go. He held me against my will, saying I would watch him take his life, because I was the reason he wanted to. He—he—" I gulped. "He cut his wrists with a box cutter. He went to work, but I need to protect myself."

"Oh my! What can we do?"

"I need a ride to the police station. Do you think Aaron can take me?"

I could hear my brother's voice echo from the background as she hollered to ask him and gave a brief reason. I could hear his shouts of profanity.

"Hey, have him wait to get me until after my mom picks up the kids," I said, cutting off his anger. "I am calling her next. Then I will call you back and tell him when to get me. Do you think he can cut me some boards to put in my windows? I will need at least six. Can he bring them when he comes?"

In the distance on their end, I heard him agree.

"Tell him twenty-two inches." I held the phone with my shoulder and the tape measure in my hand.

"They need to be twenty-two inches," she repeated.

"Since he only has his garage door opener to get inside, if I disconnect the door from the automatic opener and secure the windows so he can't pry them open, he shouldn't be able to get back in the house."

She agreed. I hung up, then I drew a breath to calm my voice before I called my mom.

Mom answered on the second ring.

"Hey, I just wanted to make sure you're still picking the kids and me up after eight?" I asked, as if nothing had changed in the plan she and I had arranged the evening prior, before any of the chaos took place.

"Yes, I will be there about a quarter after. Will that be enough time to drop the kids off at school and day care and then get you to work by nine?"

"Yes. That sounds good. Thank you!"

I didn't have time to explain what had happened, because I knew telling her would turn into a lengthy conversation. And other than me not riding with her, nothing about the plan or the time for her to pick up the kids had changed. If I told her, she would worry. She would tell my dad, and I didn't want him to get angry.

I put on my sage-colored scrubs and went into Daniel's room to wake him up for school, just as I did every other weekday morning. "Daniel, it's time to get up." Usually, I'd tap his leg until he got up. But this time I gazed at his closed eyes for what felt like hours. I closed my own eyes and inhaled the tranquility of my baby boy still sound asleep.

"Thank you for keeping him safe," I prayed. Then I tapped his leg and made my way into Ember's room, where I repeated the gaze, the breath, and the gratitude prayer over my sleeping baby girl.

After getting Ember ready, I made my way into the kitchen and halted as I heard gravel crunch beneath car tires. A lump formed inside my throat as I quietly debated who it could be. *Is it Gary Richard?* I could barely breathe as I waited for a car door to shut and someone to come in.

When a knock came at the kitchen door, I sighed in relief, knowing it couldn't be him. I opened the door and found Tabitha cradling boards in her arms.

"Aaron said to bring these to you. That way you will have them before he picks you up."

I gestured toward the wall of the garage behind her. "Let's put them over here."

She obeyed, then followed me into the kitchen.

Another car door slammed. I froze. "Who is that? Did someone come with you?"

She shook her head, her eyes wide with fear.

My heart pounded against my chest as I stared at the kitchen door's silver doorknob, which was now turning.

Gary Richard! What am I going to do?

My mother stepped through the door.

"Oh, Mom!" I said and gasped, pressing my hands to my cheeks. "You scared me! You didn't knock; I thought you were Gary Richard."

Her smile quickly turned to worry as she glanced back and forth between Tabitha and me. "What's going on?"

I lowered my voice to a loud whisper. "The kids are in the other room, and I don't have time to explain it all, but Aaron is going to take me to the police station this morning so that I can file a restraining order against Gary Richard."

Her eyes widened.

"He will take me to work after. Can you please help me get the kids' stuff ready and get them out of here so he can pick me up?"

She agreed.

I hugged Tabitha goodbye, then, along with my mom, gathered the kids' things. I kissed them goodbye, then trailed behind as they moved down the sidewalk and piled into the car. They waved as they pulled onto the road, with no clue what had taken place inside our home four hours ago, or what was about to take place. I was glad they didn't know. They were safe, and they were going to be safe.

I went into the garage and pulled the lever to disconnect the door. Then I gathered the boards and pounded them inside the window frames with my palm. I brushed my hands together and called Aaron.

"I'm ready."

We parked next to the curb in front of the station. I paused, holding the door handle, to gather my distorted thoughts. *If I open this door, there is no going back. But if I don't, there is no going forward.* I drew a deep breath and stood in the all-too-familiar station lobby where I had so often waited for Gary Richard to come out from behind the glass door after being arrested or questioned. Now I waited for something else. With eyes fixated on that same glass door, I waited for an officer to take me behind it to give my statement about the crime Gary Richard committed against me.

An officer approached and reached out his hand, greeting us with his warm smile. He led Aaron and me down a hallway, which carried the smell of the crisp morning air mixed with the musty heat coming from the vents hanging on the ceiling. He directed us toward the chairs inside a room, then he walked around the table and sat in front of us.

"What brings you in today?"

I clutched my clammy hands under the table. "I need to file a report against my husband." My eyes widened to hold back the tears. "He held me against my will last night, and I need to protect my children and me."

For what seemed like hours, I gave details of what happened as the officer encouraged me on with nods, writing my words on a paper that shouted out Offense/Incident Report in bold along the top.

"Do you want to press charges?" he asked.

I looked at Aaron. He pointed at me with his chin and offered a slight grin, causing me to exhale in relief. His support eased the slow panic building within. I turned back toward the officer. "Yes."

The officer instructed me to go directly across the street to the courthouse to file a restraining order.

Aaron and I walked across the street and down a narrow hallway lined with tables the size of elementary students' desks. I went to the lady behind the counter and told her the officer had sent us over to file a restraining order. She handed me a clipboard with papers attached, and I tucked myself in at one of the tables to fill them out.

"Hi, I'm Don," a tall, slender man with white hair said as I was still staring at the pages. "My job is to help navigate you through the court process." His voice was soothing. He felt like a friend I could say anything to. "If you need anything, I am here to help you. I am a court advocate for women of domestic violence."

I gasped silently and tried to flash a smile that I'm sure looked more bewildered than anything. "Domestic violence," he'd said. *Am I supposed to be bleeding, bruised, or sitting with bones broken to be considered a woman of domestic violence? Do I have a right to be here if I am not? Am I supposed to need something? Or ask something?* All I knew was that I just wanted to be safe. I didn't want to feel scared as I had been a few hours before, when I had no control.

Don and I talked about the report I'd given to the police and why I thought I needed an order of protection. He gently guided me until the papers were filled out and had me wait there until they said the judge would grant the ex parte and that the sheriff's department would serve Gary Richard the papers. My mind strangulated his words. *He will kill me when they serve him papers.*

Shortly after eleven, we headed back to Aaron's truck, and I reached into my purse for my phone, which I'd placed on silent mode before going into the station. My hands began to tremble when the screen revealed missed calls—eighteen from Gary Richard and five from my work. I turned toward

Aaron. "He called, Gary Richard called," I said in a brittle voice. "What should I say?"

"You can't tell him where you were. Not until he gets served with that restraining order."

I knew he was right. I couldn't tell him where I had been, but what would I say? I dialed work first.

I'd barely gotten her name out when Regina chopped off my words. "Caroline! Gary Richard has called here all morning looking for you. He wanted to know where you were. I didn't know what to say, so I told him all I knew was that you were going to be late, and I didn't know why." She took a breath. "What should I say if he calls back?"

"I'm going to call him. We just left the station, and I am on my way to work now. I should be there in about ten minutes."

I hung up the phone, and as Aaron continued to drive, my mind considered all the lies I could conjure to account for where I had been for all the hours Gary Richard had tried to reach me. *I had to help my mom. I was helping at Daniel's school. I fell back asleep.*

I swallowed the lump in my throat and dialed. With each ring, I silently pleaded for him not to answer.

"Hello."

My heart sank. "Hey, work said you called."

"Yes, several times. At work and on your cell phone. Where have you been? And why were you late?"

I straightened my shoulders to steady my voice. "Yeah, sorry, my phone has been on silent all morning. After we dropped the kids off at school, my mom had to run to the office at her work, so I told her to do that before taking me so she didn't have to backtrack. I didn't want to tell Regina that, because I knew they would be upset that I was going to be late. I'm at work now though."

"What time do you get off?" His tone sounded callous.

"Five thirty. Regina is supposed to give me a ride home, and my mom is getting the kids."

We hung up, without him ever saying what he wanted, but his tone lingered. Something seemed off, though I wasn't sure if it was coming from him or me, because I lied. I thanked Aaron for all his help and went in to work. In between helping patients, I explained to Regina more details of the day. The more I spoke of it, the more I felt as though I were describing someone else's life.

Regina pulled into my driveway at around six. The bright motion lights above the garage doors didn't turn on as they always did, so I knew something was wrong, and I thought back to his callous tone.

"Have they served him yet?" she asked.

"I don't think so. I haven't heard from him, and I think he'll call and yell at me when they do."

"I am not letting you go inside until we know what's going on with him."

I dialed Gary Richard's number and heard three tone chimes, then a robotic voice telling me that my phone was unable to make calls, because my number had been temporarily suspended. I gulped and stared wide-eyed at Regina. "I can't make calls. He's done something to my phone." Regina handed me her phone, and I dialed Gary Richard's number.

As soon as he answered, I jumped in. "Gary Richard—"

"I know, Caroline," he said harshly, interrupting me. "I know what you did this morning. You think I'm stupid. I knew when I couldn't get ahold of you that you went to the police station."

I couldn't speak. I shook my head, trying to process how he could know.

"Well, guess what?" he shouted. "You think you're so smart. Well, good luck with the police finding me. I left work today after I couldn't reach you, and they aren't ever going to find me."

"Gary Richard, stay away from the kids and me," I pleaded. "If you come home, I am calling the police. Don't do that to the kids. They will be scared."

"How do you like not having a phone?"

His smug tone sent shivers down my spine, and somehow I knew the light wasn't turning on because he had already been inside our home.

Reluctantly, Regina and I went inside the house to make sure the kids, who were still with my mom, and I would be safe. I noticed empty hangers in our closet, empty shelves and drawers in the dresser, confirming he had been there. I realized he'd used the remote to the other garage door, the one I hadn't disconnected, because I didn't think he had the remote. I went ahead and disconnected it now, and before Regina left, I checked the locks on all the doors. Then I called my mom to have her bring the kids home.

"Is everything okay?" Mom asked.

"Yes," I told her, not wanting her to worry more than I was sure she already had.

I greeted them at the door and told them we would soon be going to bed and that their daddy was staying with a friend tonight. My mom hugged me tight and said to call if I needed something and that my dad would come right over. I locked all the doors, then checked them again multiple times before and after I tucked Daniel into his bed and said our nightly prayer, "Now I lay me down to sleep."

I turned out his light and then rocked Ember to sleep on the couch while leaving the other lights on in the house. Once she was asleep, I carried her into my bedroom, because I wanted her to be close to me, where I knew she would be safe.

As we lay there, I began to feel moisture seeping through my shirt. I thought Ember must have peed her pants. Though she was potty trained, I knew accidents could happen, since she was only three. Then my shirt started feeling wetter, so I checked on Ember. She felt dry. Confused, I picked her up and placed her back on the couch. Then I went back into the bedroom and turned on the light to figure out what was going on.

I pulled back the mattress cover to reveal the water coils. I examined each one like a detective and noticed each one had been slit. Not a gash, but a simple slit down the center of each coil, done in a way that I wouldn't notice right away. I would only discover it if I lay on the bed. I knew who caused this.

Gary Richard.

Tears rose to the surface of my eyes.

How could he be so cruel?

Turning off the light, I headed back into the living room and snuggled up against Ember on the couch, hoping and praying sleep would come quickly.

The next day, my aunt called my dad, because she'd heard Gary Richard's name on the police scanner she listened to for entertainment. By that evening, Tabitha called to tell me the police had arrested him in their driveway. Apparently Gary

Richard had been in contact with the police and arranged to turn himself in there. I was able to speak to the officer, and I asked if I could pick up our car, since I was without transportation.

"As long as your name is on the registration, you're free to pick it up," he told me.

Tabitha picked me up, and when I got in, I saw the ATM transaction receipt showing that Gary Richard had withdrawn all $300 from our account. When I arrived back home, I searched deeper throughout the car to see what else was there. Under the seat, I felt something rectangular and pulled it out. It was a videotape.

Curious. Who keeps a videotape under the seat?

I took it inside and put it in our VCR.

My jaw dropped as I watched myself lying on top of our bed in a drunken state. Because of the baby-blue slacks I was wearing, I knew he'd recorded this the night of a wedding reception Gary Richard and I had attended a few years before, when I'd had a lot to drink. I watched as Gary Richard scanned my body with the lens of the camera and moved closer to me. Tears streamed down my cheeks as I watched him prop the camera on the dresser and climb next to my limp body. I shook in horror while I watched his fingertips smudge every ounce of my identity as he used my body for more than an hour as a toy.

I ripped the tape from the machine and repeatedly cut the ribbon inside it, then I broke the plastic outer casing. I covered my face in embarrassment as I fell to my knees, wondering how I had allowed this to happen. I shifted to anger that he hadn't protected me, and that I hadn't protected myself. I wondered if my body—minus my mind—was all he'd ever wanted from me. I felt dirty. Stained. Betrayed. I wondered if he *ever* saw me as something more than an object to destroy. I was glad he was behind bars. I felt broken but safe.

I wondered how this could be the man I had bonded with, the man who I'd believed made me whole, the man I'd once watched behind the glass of a bathroom mirror, wanting him to choose me, to fall in love with me, to build a home for me.

That generous man never existed, I realized. I had gotten this man instead. A man who now made me feel repulsed as I watched him do things to my body I didn't condone. Through the glass of time, his reflection had come clear. He was a man who broke trust and shattered souls.

CHAPTER 14

MEMORY

"I found a cordless handset to a phone. Why do you think Gary Richard would have that in his car?" I asked my sister-in-law, Tabitha. I had destroyed the awful videotape, but it was still on my mind.

"With him, it is hard telling. Is it one from your house?"

"No, I've never seen this before. It doesn't match any of the phones we have." I tiptoed through the kitchen to the kids' rooms to make sure they were still asleep.

"Hmm." She went silent for a moment, then I could hear her calling out to my brother. "Hey, Caroline found a cordless handset to a phone in Gary Richard's car. Why do you think he would have that in there?"

Aaron's gravelly calm voice rolled in the background. "Does he have another phone line run?"

"No." But as the word left my mouth, it was replaced with thoughts of the other night when Gary Richard had repeated the conversation I had with Tabitha. I gulped. "The other night, when he held me hostage ... somehow he knew everything we said to each other. I didn't know how he knew, but now ..."

"I bet he has one out in the garage and he listened to your conversation," Aaron said. I was obviously now on speakerphone. "Look at the walls. If he has one, there would be a wire plugged into a jack. Look for a wire running up from the floor."

I nearly ran into the garage, and moving as fast as lightning bolts, my eyes flashed to the ceiling, the walls, and over by his workbench. I placed my palms on the frosted concrete and angled my head toward the area where the wall intersected with the floor. "There *is* a wire. Oh no!" I shouted. "He has a phone! He has a secret phone!"

"Do you see the base?" Aaron said. "He'd have to have a way to charge the handset."

I pushed my body off the ground, being careful not to lose sight of the thin oatmeal-colored wire charting its course from the jack into the vertical beads of the paneling and to the wooden beams over my head. Heavy gray tape wound around one beam. "I found the base. It's taped to the rafters."

They offered a few gasps but mostly remained silent, which said more than words could. I wondered if Tabitha also felt a spring tightening in her stomach.

"Oh, Caroline," she finally sputtered, as though reading my thoughts.

I stared arrow-straight at his car. "Let me call you back. I need to see if the camcorder bag is in his car. That's the only thing he took that I want to find."

After I hung up, I quickly opened the trunk and began rummaging through the items there. A jack, jumper cables, some quarts of oil, and a couple blankets and portable chairs. Blood began pulsating in my ears louder than my thoughts.

Where is it? I turned the crate filled with cleaners on its side, and the reflective emergency vest fell to the floor. *Where is it?* I slammed the trunk, eyes full of water, throat closed.

What did he do with it? What did he do with our memories? Our children's first steps, first words, the school Christmas program where Daniel was missing his front teeth and proudly singing out of tune. The videos reflecting the sparkles in our children's eyes as they opened the presents Santa left behind or blew out the candles on top of their birthday cakes, which they always did twice, because we always sang the "Happy Birthday" song two times. Family traditions were captured on that camcorder, along with a million random moments in between. What had he done with them all?

Sliding down the bumper, feeling defeat, I turned my head and fixed my eyes on the exhaust that yesterday released a plume of smoke into the biting winter air as Gary Richard pulled out from our drive. I'd felt sure of my direction then. Now I felt lost in the clouds formed by the coldness of his deceit.

Whose husband keeps a secret phone? Was anything about our life together real, or was it all a lie? Why is this always happening to me?

I needed to find the camcorder and the black bag that held our tapes, because I desperately needed to breathe in the laughter, the smiles, the memories—the things that were sweet—to replace the bitterness suffocating me.

With my palms on the floor, I pushed myself up, my legs and mind too exhausted to do anything except grab towels and extra blankets to layer on the bed so I could fall into it, hoping I would drift quickly into the land of dreams. Done fighting with reality, I kept whispering, "I am tired, so very tired." A tear rolled down my cheek.

The morning came, although it felt like I had just closed my eyes when my phone rang.

"This is a collect call from . . ." The recording crackled and paused, then Gary Richard's voice announced his name, followed by more crackles and finishing with "an inmate at the county jail." I stared out the window, listening intently for instructions for accepting the call, though I wasn't certain I wanted to.

"Hey." Gary Richard's voice was as crisp as the brown winter grass looked.

I paused, making space for a response, wondering how he could sound as though nothing had changed when everything had. *Does he remember about the restraining order? Is he going to apologize for slicing our bed?*

Anger bubbled in my chest as I considered what I might say—*"Do you still think I'm boring in bed? It didn't seem so on the tape." "When you smirked as your fingers navigated the stretch marks, which joke did you recite? The one about my road map or the place where semitrucks could park?"* Just when I thought I could let it all burst from my mouth, I couldn't.

"Since I am locked up, you should go get my car so you have something to drive."

Like a riptide, the sound of his voice changed the current in my mind, and somehow I no longer wanted to confront him about anything, including the secret phone, because I needed his loving voice to stay.

"I already did. I spoke to the officer last night, who said as long as my name was on the registration, I could take it."

"Okay. Well, that's good. Also, if you need anything of mine, my stuff is at Emily's apartment."

My jaw clenched at the sound of her name. *Emily,* a woman he knew from high school. *Emily,* our former neighbor's friend whom I once confronted Gary Richard about when I wondered why she cracked her door whenever the dirt bike he played around on fired up in our driveway. *Emily*, the mother of a daughter whom Gary Richard had once coached in Little League soccer. *Emily*, the grieving widow our hearts ached for as she mourned the unexpected death of her husband.

"Is that where you have been staying?" I choked out the question.

"Yes."

The walls felt as though they were closing in. *How could he go there?*

I knew he wouldn't stay at his dad's because of his dad's excessive alcohol use, which made him belligerent. I knew he wouldn't stay with his siblings because of the instability in their lives, due to their criminal backgrounds. I didn't know where I expected him to go, but it certainly was not to Emily's.

"Is that where our camcorder is?" I blurted out.

"Yes."

I let loose a sigh, taking time on the exhale, hoping he would explain why he had gone to Emily's. Hoping he would reassure me that they were just friends. Hoping he would know I wasn't okay with that decision.

"You can go pick it up," he said calmly. "I spoke to her earlier, and she knows you have my permission to pick up any of my stuff."

Oddly, his words made my heart warm.

I didn't want him back, but I didn't want Emily to have him either. While I didn't like the things he did to me, I didn't want to confront him, because I needed the comfort of him on my side—and right now he was. "Okay, I will get in contact with her later today and pick it up. I need the camcorder for Christmas morning."

"It makes me sad I won't be there to watch them open their presents."

His sudden melancholic tone triggered the hamster wheel of my guilt. I was the reason he was locked up. Before I could think of what I was saying, the words came out. "I'm sorry, Gary Richard." My heart ached. "I know the kids will want to talk to you. Can you call later and talk with them? You're still their father, and I won't keep them away from you."

"Can I talk to them now?"

"They're still sleeping, but maybe you can try again later?" I said delicately, making sure not to crack the eggshells my emotions were walking on.

A short time later, after the kids woke up, I patted the sandy carpet on Daniel's floor while Ember nestled between my crisscrossed legs.

"Come sit beside me. I need to talk to you about your dad." The innocence in Daniel's nine-year-old eyes washed across my heart like waves on the shore. I knew whatever I said, he would believe. "You know how if you do something you're not supposed to, there is a consequence? Like when you get grounded, and I take your video games away?"

He nodded as three-year-old Ember started bouncing like a puppy across the room.

"Sometimes when you're older and make a bad choice, if the choice is really bad, you have to go to jail. Well, Daddy made a bad choice." I clasped his hands. "Daddy had to go to jail."

As his eyes lowered, I leaned down to catch them. "Hey, you will still get to talk to him, though, because he is going to call you and your sister."

Though he didn't ask me anything, his eyes betrayed that he was wondering if I'd told him the truth.

I wrapped my arms around him and half smiled at Ember, who was trying to reach for the lava lamp I had pushed back on Daniel's dresser, hoping she would forget it was there.

I was happy that the moment seemed normal to her, that her world hadn't felt as if it stopped, as mine often did. But I was envious, too, at the way she didn't stop reaching for something even though she couldn't see it. She didn't stand there questioning what was real, as I often did.

I inhaled slowly, raising my thoughts to God. I hadn't been back to church since the day Pastor Bob asked us to form the circle and pray for my family, which was more than three weeks before.

Please, God, let the children be okay. Please help me be strong and know what to say. Please, take the confusion away.

I clutched Daniel's shoulder and pushed his body from mine, then cupped his face in my hands. "Look at me."

His teary eyes met mine.

"I know this is hard to understand, but we are not responsible for your dad's choices. We didn't do anything wrong. We don't get to use it as an excuse to make bad choices. You still have to be good at school and home. I know you are upset, I know you feel scared, I know you miss your dad, but we are going to be okay, and your sister and I will always be here."

His words stayed tucked behind his almost smile.

I gently wiped across the trails sliding down his cheeks. "Come on, let's go eat some breakfast."

This day, four days before Christmas, we moved through our day as if we didn't have any place to be or anything to do. School was on holiday break. Our garage held wrapped gifts that Santa would deliver on Christmas morning, adding to the small pile already sitting beneath the multicolored decorated tree in the living room.

I called Emily around five at the number Gary Richard gave.

She answered on the first ring. "Hello." Her voice sounded pleasant.

"Hey, Emily, this is Gary Richard's wife, Caroline. He said I could come to your apartment and get his things. I'd like to pick those up today. When can I come?" I said, leaving no breathing room between words.

"You are welcome to come get anything you need. I will be home all evening. Do you know how to get to my place?"

"No," I snapped as I threw open the drawer to grab paper, then scratched down the address she gave.

After we hung up, I arranged for my mom to keep the kids and drove to Emily's apartment after picking up Tabitha to go with me. We pulled into the driveway and made our way up the steps, where Emily grinned and pushed open her door to let us in.

"Where are his things?" I said in a slow panic, which eased in when I saw Emily's toddler running toward us.

Emily reached down and removed Gary Richard's hat from her daughter's head, revealing her eyes. "She keeps putting on his hats."

The room blurred as I followed her. Gary Richard's shoes were lined up along the wall, and his hats sat in unequal rows across the window seat.

"His stuff is in here." She pointed with her chin as she turned on the light. "I took it out of the closet and laid it there so it would be easier for you."

She left the room as Tabitha and I looked at each other, then back at the soft heap of rich, colorful shirts mounted on the bed. My lips parted in surprise.

"Are you taking them?" Tabitha asked.

I nodded. "And that." I pointed to the dresser, where glass cologne bottles decorated the front of the camcorder bag.

The shirts draped like limp noodles around our arms, and the hangers smacked against each other as we stretched them across the back seat. The crisp linen and plump polyester mound grew higher as we moved methodically back and forth from the room to the car, while Emily observed silently from the couch. Over and over, back and forth we went, until every trace of him slowly disappeared from her home.

"We got it all. Thanks," I blurted through the uncertain smile I gave, then headed out the door.

I could feel the flush of color warm my cheeks as I turned toward Tabitha. "That was weird. It looked like he lived there. Did you see the little girl wearing his hat?"

Tabitha's brows tipped up. "I know." She clutched my hand.

After I dropped her off, I piled his clothes in the back of the SUV my dad had towed back to my house after being unable to fix it. I held each shirt to my nose, inhaling the woodsy scent longer and longer until the memory of him covered me like the mist in the forest.

I wanted to stay where my mind drifted seamlessly between the land of dreams and reality, but I couldn't. I knew things had changed. I knew he was a cycle I struggled to break. I knew I couldn't live with him, but I didn't know how to live without him.

As the days rolled past, the kids and I celebrated Christmas as we always did, beginning with baking cookies on Christmas Eve and leaving them on the counter for Santa, next to a cold glass of milk. Then we headed outside for our most recent tradition of sprinkling "reindeer food" across the grass while our teeth chattered and our bones froze. And of course, early Christmas morning, I awoke and grabbed the video camera to capture more memories as the kids exited their rooms with half-opened eyes and dashed toward the tree.

"Did Santa come?" I asked from behind the camera, zooming in on the kids' faces and the presents under the tree.

Though Gary Richard wasn't with us, the day was still magical, as Christmases had always been as far as I could remember.

"Mom, look! Look at this." Daniel's eyes glistened as he waved the computer box over his head.

His dimpled smile filled the lens as the camera moved like molasses toward him. "How awesome. Santa brought you a computer?"

A computer. Those words drifted like a familiar melody from the speaker of memory weeks earlier when Gary Richard excitedly came home with the Black Friday deal he'd camped out to get.

"I can't wait to see his face on Christmas morning," he'd said. "I'm so happy I went out there to get it."

In an instant, I returned to the day I had stared at *our computer* and the memory of what I had seen while he was out purchasing this one for Daniel. A chill passed through my bones. *How could he do that to me? To us?* I heard the wrapping paper crumple and managed to pull my mind out of the past and onto Daniel's beaming smile. He packed the wrapping paper like a snowball between his palms and caressed the box now lying at his side. The camera traced every ounce of joy beaming from his face. Clearly this was his most treasured gift.

Once again the seesaw of my emotions changed direction. I could feel myself growing sympathetic toward Gary Richard again, knowing the one who made this moment possible wasn't here to see it.

How could I have done that to him—make him miss this special memory? How could I have done that to all of us? I could feel my eyes tearing up again. *I am sorry, Gary Richard, so very sorry for the memory you aren't getting to see.*

CHAPTER 15

EVIDENCE

"Start from the beginning."

For the second time, I heard Sergeant Frank Long say the words, in a husky tone that fit well with his thick neck and bulging stomach.

Breathe, Caroline. Just breathe, I silently told myself while continuing to fix my eyes on the white paper horizon stretched across his earthy-colored desk.

"When did you meet your husband?"

I shifted my legs in the chair as the concrete walls seemed to move closer, causing chills to snake down my back. Although I knew the answer, I couldn't loosen the fear constricting my throat to say it. All I could think was *How did I get here?*

Scene after scene replayed, revealing answer after answer.

I got here because . . . my brother, Aaron, spoke with Sergeant Long a couple of days after Christmas, who informed him there was still an ongoing investigation surrounding the allegations the teenage girl made against Gary Richard in early November, roughly eight weeks earlier.

I got here because . . . Aaron told him I had printed evidence the day after Thanksgiving of Gary Richard communicating with teenage girls on the computer.

I got here because . . . the day after Sergeant Long spoke with Aaron, he reached out to me asking if I would be willing to come in at eight the following morning, December 29, to state what I saw, in hopes it could strengthen the victim's case.

I got here because . . . I knew this girl, and I cared about her and her family.

I got here because . . . I believed her.

"How old were you?"

"Sixteen." I finally raised my eyes toward the heavy pecking sound coming from the keyboard.

"How did you meet him? Did you go to school with him?" he asked, although by the way his eyes rolled over the top of his glasses as he tilted his head forward, I felt he already knew.

Maybe he did. Sergeant Frank Long had known me before I was born, twenty-seven years now. He and my dad worked together for many years at the jail, where they started as deputies. Though my dad left to work at a mattress factory that paid more money, Frank stayed on with the department and, years later, became a sergeant and an investigator with the sex crimes and crimes against children unit. Growing families, time, and career paths had sent the men their separate ways. And although we didn't go over to their house for dinner parties, as we had when I was seven, Frank's wife and my mom would occasionally catch up in the aisle of the neighborhood grocery store, which was only blocks from both their houses.

So admitting this to Frank felt as though I was admitting it to my dad. I knew I needed to, but it came at great embarrassment. "No, he's older than me and didn't live in this town growing up."

Frank's cell phone rang, strangling my last words. He

checked the ID and pointed his finger in the air, as if to tell me to hold on. "I need to take this."

I nodded, but from the way his hand swallowed his phone, I understood he wasn't asking or waiting for my permission.

Trying not to listen to his conversation, I traced with the tip of my shoe the specks of gray that looked like tinfoil confetti trapped inside the floor tiles.

"Okay. Did you get it back?" Frank asked. Silence followed, except for the faint clicks of metal coming from somewhere behind me. Finally Frank spat out, "Tell them to give it back, or we will put a trace on it, and they'll be dealing with me." He let out a loud sigh. "Some boys over at the high school are messing with Kevin at practice," he shouted to the deputy tucked between two file cabinets across the room. "They took his phone and are telling him they don't have it; they think they're funny."

The deputy smirked as he looked up from the beige folder he was holding. "They don't want to mess with him or his dad."

"You got that right," Frank said, hypnotically rocking his head back and forth as if he were in a trance, focused only on the secret thoughts of what he would do to anyone messing with his son.

I didn't mind the break from being the center of Frank's attention; it allowed me to relax a little. I could see *Frank*, not the sergeant but *Frank the father*. I could see the love he held for his son inside his deep brown eyes.

"Now, where were we?" he said, pulling his chair closer to his desk and focusing again on me. "Ah, yes. How did you meet him?"

"Some boys I went to high school with lived with him."

His eyes narrowed. "How did they meet him?"

I swallowed, knowing it would sound awkward, because when I first met Gary Richard, I thought it was awkward that they lived with their boss. I thought it strange that his circle of friends was the same as mine—until I got to know his personality, so youthful and carefree, with days filled with adventures like Peter Pan. After that, I hadn't given his living situation a second thought.

"He was their manager at a fast-food restaurant in town."

"I see." Frank tipped his chin up, then quickly grabbed his chirping phone. The corners of his mouth grew into the fold of his cheeks, and I knew the bullies had given Kevin back his phone. "You have a son with him, correct?"

"Yes!" A smile washed over me as thoughts of the children turned me like flowers toward the sun. "And a daughter."

"You were younger when you had your son, correct?"

Instantly, I wilted as shame prickled like needles under my skin. I wondered what Frank had thought ten years ago when the gossip of Ted's teenage daughter getting knocked up filled his home. *Did he shake his head and make a vow that wouldn't happen to his babies? Did he share in my parents' sense of doom? Or did he close his brown eyes in disgust?* My eyes fell back toward the confetti tile, which had lost its sparkle.

"Yes, I was in high school when I had him."

"How old were you when you got pregnant?"

"Sixteen. I got pregnant at the end of my junior year."

For the next several hours, Frank tapped the keys repeatedly, sometimes so fast it sounded like horses galloping across a hard surface. He wanted to know the exact month I met

Gary Richard, the month I discovered I was pregnant, how old I was when we got married, as if he was plotting points on the timeline of our relationship.

"Caroline, as I told you on the phone, we have been investigating Gary Richard for the last eight weeks, and including the teen who initially came forward, five girls are willing to testify that he has victimized them in some way."

My heart curled into a ball and felt as though it just flung itself against the concrete wall behind him.

"The prosecutor is still determining what she will charge him with, because there are a few things she can. One victim indicated she had sexual relations with Gary Richard when she was fourteen. He was twenty-six. He could face charges in two different counties since she alleged he had sex with her at her aunt's home, located in the county south of us. The other house belonged to a family friend who lives in the same neighborhood as your cousins. That's how he met her, by the way."

I couldn't speak. Instead all I could do was cower behind a wall of silence, hoping if I stayed quiet enough, he would go away, and I could safely flee.

"When I heard you went to the station and then I read a copy of your statement, I hoped you would be willing to testify against him. I want to move quickly on this case, because I want to charge him before he's released so he isn't back out on the streets. Your statement today helps. I want to use the papers you printed to establish a pattern of behavior to help strengthen one of the other girls' testimony."

I pushed my fingers through my hair as I thought back to a spring morning in April 2006 when I had looked at a puddle of sunlight on the kitchen floor as I made my way to the coffee pot. Catching a glimpse of a paper on the counter,

I'd pivoted on my heel and picked it up. Gary Richard's handwritten note started with *I am sorry.*

He was sorry for not coming directly home after he left the evening before to fight a house fire with the volunteer fire department. He was sorry for not telling me he had been chatting with my friend Molly's teenage sister after she reached out to him online. He was sorry he met her in the parking lot of a grade school after the fire, because she'd begged him to meet her in person finally.

His apologies turned to pleas that he didn't do anything wrong, only met her to talk.

I moved my eyes down the paper to an explanation that sounded true: *When I pulled in, her friends jumped up from the back seat, shouting out the windows that I was busted and they were telling my wife.* I had silently cried out, *Not again. Why is it always something with him?*

"Caroline," I heard Sergeant Long say, and his brown eyes drew me back to the present. "Do you still have the papers?"

"I . . . I did, but this morning when I went to get them from the cabinet above the refrigerator, they were gone."

His eyes dropped, heavy with disappointment.

I understood that. I was disappointed too—in Gary Richard, for his behavior patterns, and in me, for not seeing them sooner. "I don't know for sure, but I assume Gary Richard found them the day I went to the police station."

Frank stood. "Caroline, I appreciate you coming. Sorry I kept you here so long, and I got a little distracted earlier with my son. Tell your dad I said hi."

I walked down the hallway and out the glass doors that faced my car, parked along the street, hoping my words would bring some relief and support to those girls. The old brick buildings slipped by my windows as I made my way toward the four-way stop by the bridge downtown. My phone rang. It was an unknown number, but somehow I knew it was Frank.

"Caroline, have you gotten very far?"

"No, just a few blocks away, almost to the bridge."

"I realized after you left, I didn't ask you to sign your statement."

"Oh, I can pull back around. Be there in a minute."

Frank handed me a silver pen and pointed toward the bottom of the paper he had lined up at the edge of his desk. I signed, then shook my purse searching for my keys, which I'd dropped in there on my way into the building.

Frank cleared his throat as he scooped the signed statement from the table and held it to his chest. "When you left, I called over and spoke with the prosecutor."

I nodded, still fishing for the keys in my purse.

"She is going to charge Gary Richard, but not for what you think."

I tried to anticipate what words would follow, still distracted by the jangle of keys I couldn't locate.

"She is going to charge him for you."

"What?" I snapped to attention immediately, feeling the blood drain from my face.

"She wants to charge him for statutory rape against you, because you were sixteen when he had sex with you, and he was twenty-four."

Swirls of confusion twisted in my head. "What? But we are married. I am his wife."

Frank leaned forward. I could see the divide of part detective and part father in his eyes. "The only difference between you and the other girls is that he married you."

My eyes burned with hatred. *How could he say that to me? Didn't marriage make everything okay and legal?*

It didn't make sense. Nine years ago, our marriage may have been Gary Richard's ploy, but how could Sergeant Long say our being together was a crime? Did he not understand the way my blue eyes washed over Gary Richard's golden-tanned skin, pulling pieces of him into me like the sand going into the sea? Did he not care that the smells of amber and citrus cascading from Gary Richard's coal-black hair made me feel safe and calm as his body pressed against mine? Did it not matter that I had traced every inch of Gary Richard's manly reflection as he stood in front of the large rectangular mirror?

"Caroline, they are charging him for the crime committed against you, because you have evidence he can't deny. With the other girls, it's only their word against his." No longer did I see or care to search for *Frank the father* in his eyes. "You can take it up with the prosecutor, but I will tell you in the case of child sex crimes, like statutory rape, the state can choose to prosecute without you. They don't need the victim's consent to charge these crimes, and they have up to twenty years from your eighteenth birthday to do so."[2]

I inhaled a deep breath and blew out slowly, trying to buy time to find words to hurl at him because of his betrayal. Had this been his intention all along?

Sergeant Long moved closer, resting his body against the desk.

---

[2] In 2018 the state statue was amended to allow for prosecutions of unlawful sexual offenses involving a person eighteen years of age or under to be commenced at any time.

What else can he possibly say? Hasn't he already said enough? He's told me I am a victim, although I don't feel like one. I do feel afraid. Was coming here a mistake? He tricked me into signing. He told me I'm just another of the many females, and as Gary Richard's wife, that makes me sick.

Cradling my stomach, I hoped my arms would shield me from the onslaught of his words. They didn't. They couldn't.

He proceeded, "Caroline, you have physical evidence of his crime . . . because you have a son."

CHAPTER 16

DADDY'S HANDS

I squeezed the wheel of Gary Richard's blue Honda as I wove between cars and faded white lines, heading south across the bridge over the river. Navigating roads, exit ramps, and the confusion of what just happened—wondering how to outrun all the words racing through my mind since I walked out of Sergeant Long's office ten minutes before.

Crime. Victim. Evidence. Son . . . Crime. Victim. Evidence. Son . . .

Searching for a place to escape the information stuck in my head, I drove toward the only place I knew I would be safe. Safe from betrayal. Safe from the emotions ripping me apart. Safe from the words repeating like the rows of identical orange storage units I passed heading down the street to my parents' home.

I wandered up the steps of the porch, my fingers carving into the grooves of the white spindles wrapping around it, turning my mind into a kaleidoscope of childhood events and memories of my daddy's hands. Hands that repaired the poles broken by kids swinging on them. Hands that spanked, slicing my bottom with burning pain—a consequence for misbehaving. And yet they were also hands that protected me. Hands that were reliable. Hands that I let go of to grab hold of Gary Richard's. Hands that held mine when Gary Richard let go of me.

Puffs of white floral and citrus scents floated like clouds out of the dryer vent over the wicker chair, awakening my senses to the present. Mom's car was missing from the drive, so I knew she was still at work. That was okay. She wasn't the one I needed to see right now.

I slowly inhaled and exhaled as I pressed the doorbell. Within moments, I heard my dad's lumbering footsteps.

"Who is it?" His thunderous voice drowned out his steps.

"Dad, it's me." My voice cracked.

Immediately the door swung open, and his hands pulled my frail body—now shaking with long, racking sobs—into his arms, holding me as tight as a butterfly inside a cocoon. I couldn't escape from his shield of love, nor did I want to. He was the only man I could trust.

"F-Frank said they are charging—" Sobs strangled my words.

"It's okay. I know."

Pushing my body from his, I dried my face with my shirtsleeve before dropping onto the couch and curling into a fetal position.

"Frank called me about thirty minutes ago, and so did Aaron," Dad said, sinking swiftly into the recliner next to the couch, causing the corners of Grandma's knitted blanket covering the top to wave in the air. "They both told me what happened."

My heart jumped from sadness back to the anger of betrayal. "But, Dad, I don't understand. Why would Frank do that? I went there to help the victims, not to become one. I went there to bring evidence, not have him and the prosecutor tell me I gave birth to it."

He nodded compassionately.

"Frank said I could call and talk with the prosecutor, but with statutory rape, the state can prosecute without the victim's consent."

"Are you going to?"

I sighed and wiped my runny nose. "Yeah, just not today. And the office is closed on Monday for New Year's, so maybe on Tuesday. I have to talk to her to explain that I'm not a victim. That it wasn't like that with us."

"Like what?"

My heart jumped again, from the pain of betrayal to sadness over what no one seemed able to see or understand. "It's like they're saying Daniel shouldn't be here. How could they insinuate that? Dad, he's a good boy, you know that! He's such a good boy." I buried my face into the cushion, interrupting the tears to draw a breath. Then slowly I sat up. "He's not a product of something evil or wrong. He's smart, amazing, and kind—not the evidence of a crime. He is my son. He's our Daniel."

"I know it's confusing, but that's not what they are saying. You have to look at it from their side. Their job is to look for the charge they can prove, and when there is evidence leaving no doubt he committed a crime, that's the one they will use."

"But if they charge him for me, he will never have to admit what he did to them."

"I hear you, but if they charge him for the others and he pleads not guilty, it goes to trial."

"Okay, what's wrong with that?"

"It's their word against his."

I let out an exasperated sigh. "You can't tell me a jury wouldn't believe them. There is more than one girl!"

"I understand what you're saying, but you know first-hand what it is like to go through a jury trial. Many things can happen. Witnesses become afraid to testify, or if they do, they buckle under the pressure of cross-examination. Emotions can cause witnesses to contradict their original statements. With so many unknowns, they aren't going to risk going to trial when they already have a charge he will plead guilty to. He can't fight what the evidence shows. He can't deny Daniel is his son when they can easily collect DNA to prove it."

I felt sick, unsure if it was from my ragged breath, the truth of his words, or both. "Can I ask you something?"

He looked at me with warm brown eyes.

"Frank said the only difference between the other girls and me is that he married me. Do you think that's true?"

He turned his head as if searching the wall to find the answer, then brushed his cheeks for a few seconds before turning back to me. "Yes."

I chewed my bottom lip, trying to gain control of my breath.

"Hon, I know you may not be able to see it right now, but someday you will."

I stared straight at my dad, not noticing him at all. Whose side was he on? Whose side was I on? I came here to be mended, hoping he would make my mind feel *whole*, but as I kissed him goodbye, I felt confused and guilty.

Guilty for what happened to those girls. Guilty that I didn't go to the police department after Thanksgiving. Guilty that I couldn't see myself as one of them. Guilty for the shock I knew Gary Richard would feel when he heard about the charges. Guilty that I couldn't see in him what Frank, the prosecutor, and my dad so clearly did. Guilty for waiting hours after I left my dad's to pick up my kids from my sister. Guilty for emptily moving through the evening routine of a mother.

My heart was splitting between anger and sadness as I laid my head on the pillow, wondering why my life always left me feeling broken, like a bucket with holes.

Two days later, on New Year's Eve 2006, I stared at the ringing phone, debating if I should answer. After all, what would I say to Gary Richard if I did? I knew he was calling collect from jail to wish the kids a Happy New Year and that he would want to know what we were doing. I knew I didn't have to answer his questions but would because it kept the peace. I knew he had planned to plead guilty at his upcoming court date for the domestic assault charge stemming from the night he held me hostage. I also knew he had no clue he would soon face charges of statutory rape.

After another ring, I answered.

"Hey, what are you and the kids doing tonight?"

"I'm getting ready to take them to Regina's. She said she would keep both of them this year so Ember can still have her New Year's Eve tradition at her house."

"I am sure they're excited. What are you doing?"

"I haven't decided yet. Mom said I could go over to Uncle Jerry's. He is having a party for the family in his garage since we're not hosting ours this year."

"That's good. Can I talk to the kids before you leave?"

"Yeah, but before you do . . . I've got to tell you something." I headed into the garage to sit in the car so the kids couldn't overhear the conversation. "Sergeant Long with the sheriff's department called me after reading the statement I made against you that day I went to the station." I closed my eyes to draw a breath, hoping he had information to finish the sentence as I exhaled.

"Did you talk to him?" he snapped.

"Yes, he asked me if I would come to talk about what I saw on your computer." My lips drew back in a snarl. "Where are the papers I printed?"

"What papers?" He didn't need to answer; I heard it in the smug tone. "What did you say to him, Caroline?" He was now scolding me like a child.

"What does it matter?" I shouted back in a voice as thunderous as my dad's. "I told him what I saw, and he asked how old I was when I got pregnant with Daniel. I told him. Gary Richard, they have been investigating you since the day they were in our drive, but I guess you knew that since Frank told me they seized your work computer before Thanksgiving. Is that why you didn't feel like being around anyone that day?"

"I can't believe you talked to them. I can't believe you did that to me."

"Did that to *you*! You have done this to you. This isn't my fault; I went there to help those girls because I don't believe you anymore."

"Caroline, I am not arguing with you. Other people need to use the phone. Tell the kids I said Happy New Year."

My hands squeezed into fists as I let the phone fall into my lap. I regretted confronting him. Regina was waiting, and the kids were waiting. I didn't have time to be sad or mad; nobody had time for that.

The year changed, and just days after the kids celebrated with Regina, I went into her office to speak with the prosecutor, who was returning my call, while Regina helped take care of my patients at the front desk.

"Hi, Mrs. Downey. This is Carol Langdon, the prosecutor on your case. How can I help you?"

"I am trying to understand why you're charging Gary Richard for me and why you wouldn't charge him for the other girls. I'm his wife."

"When we investigate cases, we gather evidence so that charges are supported. In your case, you have DNA evidence that's indisputable. There is a crime here, Mrs. Downey."

"Are you saying my son is a crime? He isn't a crime. He's such a good boy." I could feel my voice becoming shaky.

"I am sure he is. This isn't about your son. This is about a crime committed against you."

"I am not his victim. I'm his wife," I repeated.

"Mrs. Downey, I understand this doesn't make sense to you, but we have filed statutory rape charges against Mr. Downey. You can fill out a non-prosecution letter. However, the state can and will proceed with the charges because you were a minor."

"But what about all the others? If you charge him for me, he will never have to face what he has done. He will just tell everyone he got locked up for having sex with his wife, the mother of his children. He will become the victim."

"Mrs. Downey, as part of the plea bargain this county is offering him, if he pleads guilty to the crime against you, he will face charges only for that and none of the others. However, the prosecutor in Lubbock County has said he is preparing to charge Mr. Downey for the crimes taking place in his county, where he had intercourse with one of the other victims. So he will be facing two counts of statutory rape, one for each county."

I rubbed the back of my neck and slowly blew out my cheeks. I didn't know how to respond, nor did I feel it would make a difference if I did. I knew what he did to the others was wrong and that he should face the consequences of his actions. I could accept that. But how could I accept what they said happened to me?

"Mrs. Downey."

My shoulders slumped. I didn't have the energy to hear something else. But she continued. "We are going to need to get a DNA swab on your son. Just in case Mr. Downey tries to deny he is the father."

The rise of anger straightened my spine like grass in the spring. "He wouldn't ... Never!" Then the thought of Daniel, a month away from turning ten, getting swabbed cut through my voice like a sickle. "He wo-wouldn't. He won't de-deny Dan-Daniel." I fell back in the chair.

I ended the call with Mrs. Langdon, only partially hearing the rest of her words, something about someone getting in contact with me to make arrangements.

A few days later, a deputy with the sheriff's department called to ask when he could come to collect the swab. I arranged to meet him the following evening at the end of the driveway at my brother's home, to avoid becoming the subject of neighborhood gossip.

I headed one mile west around the block to my brother's driveway, parallel to the creek. What could I tell Daniel to explain why we were going there?

My mouth curved into a smile at the sight of Daniel and Ember in the back seat. Their eyes were growing wider at the view of my brother's house. I knew from their glances that they thought they were going over to play with my nieces.

After I parked, I half turned in my seat. "Daniel, your dad is sick at the jail," I said. "He's okay, but you see that cop car?" I nodded my head toward outside Ember's window.

After unbuckling his seat belt to get a better view through the tinted window, Daniel nodded.

"Well, his name is Dustin, and he knows your dad and me."

Pinning my eyes to his, I knew no matter what lie I told, it would be his truth.

"You know when I take you to the doctor's office when your throat hurts, and they stick that swab in your throat? Well, Dustin came here to do that. He needs to swab inside your mouth to make sure you don't get sick too."

As Daniel and I stepped out of the car, I looked at my sweet, innocent daughter. "We'll be right back, okay?" She nodded.

Dustin greeted us with a smile. He was holding a clear plastic bag. He greeted Daniel kindly, then held a long white tip in the air as he explained to Daniel that he would place it inside his mouth and rub for a minute.

Daniel listened as though he were taking a test for science class. When instructed, he complied, stretching open his mouth wide.

He's such a good boy. I thought back to all the conversations I'd had with my son as we drove to doctor's appointments over the past nine years. I would always prep him for shots that never seemed to bother him as much as they bothered me.

"All done!" Dustin said. Daniel closed his mouth, and Dustin tucked the swab into the bag.

"Okay, Daniel, let's go home."

Daniel and Ember offered me puzzled looks. I knew they wondered why we weren't going inside my brother's house so they could play. I knew one day I would have to explain, but how would I do that? How could a mother keep her son's identity from being skewed when he found out his DNA was labeled and used as evidence against his father? How could I accept I was a victim without rejecting my marriage's validity or my son's legality? How could I explain to them I was a crime victim, and a wife, and a mother?

How could I do that to children when at age twenty-seven, I couldn't even understand?

How will I ever explain that I am the reason they cuffed their daddy's hands?

CHAPTER 17

THE FRAME

In January 2007, the prosecuting attorney's office officially filed statutory rape charges against Gary Richard, and with the help of an employee hardship fund at my work, I was able to hire an attorney to file divorce papers.

Things were changing as we entered February. Daniel turned ten, and Gary Richard's collect calls from jail grew shorter and less frequent. Simultaneously, some things remained the same. We filled cellophane bags with candy to hand out at school on Valentine's Day, as usual. Ember was still three. And as we moved into the last week of the month, I turned to Channel 11 to watch the six o'clock news, as I had done every night that week, while fixing dinner.

Over the sizzle of the hamburger meat I was cooking, I heard Jodi, the nightly news anchor, start her report. "A local man facing charges for statutory rape will appear in court tomorrow."

My head jerked up. There plastered on the television screen was Gary Richard's mug shot. I rushed toward the set and traced the oversized letters spelling out his name as the sizzle of grease and Jodi's voice grew distant.

Is this real? How can it be?

Like trusted friends, local news anchors Bill and Jodi entered my home, giving me the rundown on area crime, regional gatherings, upcoming weather. Within minutes they'd have my eyes rolling at the people being arrested or going to court, or clutching my chest as they reported on car wrecks and tragic deaths. In just one half hour, they could have me—and the rest of our community—clinging to their sacred words to determine what or who was evil, right, wrong, or good. But tonight, the news had only been on for less than five minutes, and their top story crushed me.

How do I respond while my life is broadcast across the air?

I blinked until Jodi's porcelain skin came into view, then followed the outline of her dusty-rose lips as they unearthed truths surrounding Gary Richard's upcoming February court appearance.

Fury exploded in my mind. *Shut up, Jodi, shut up! Why are you doing this to my family? Don't you know parents are watching from Daniel's school? Don't you know I haven't told everyone about what we've gone through these past few months? Don't you know how people judge? Please don't do this, Jodi, please just shut up!*

But as though she were talking directly to me, I felt Jodi's words shout back, "Downey is accused of having sexual relations with a sixteen-year-old—"

My body froze. *What's the world saying about my family as they prepare to eat their dinner? Did they roll their eyes or clutch their chests? Say their kids aren't allowed to play with mine? What happens when Daniel becomes a teenager with a girlfriend? Will another family trust us with their daughter? Or when Ember grows into a teenager, will our home be forbidden to her circle of friends? Do they wonder if I knew what my husband was doing and to whom? Is my family's reputation too dirty to become clean?*

"—whom he later married." Jodi stared directly at me as she finished her sentence.

Her accusatory tone sent shivers down my spine. I was dirt. Unclean. The bad one in this report was me.

It wasn't the first time I watched condemnation swirl in someone's eyes, though each time it caught me by surprise. And this . . . this was what I feared. It was the prediction I'd made to the prosecutor, my dad, and Sergeant Long, and it came true every time I ran into our friends or family. They'd ask questions, trying to find out what was going on with Gary Richard or confirm if rumors they heard were true. I'd explain he was facing a statutory rape charge, and they'd gasp. And I'd stammer trying to make a long story short but give enough details about the other girls to prove he was in the wrong. Then I'd say, "They are charging him with me."

Instantly they'd bow their heads—not to pray for justice, but because they didn't know what to say to the wife who betrayed her husband. The fake smiles shone in disgust as each person walked away with a downward gaze, confirming that I should hold my head in shame. I then would look on while my prediction replayed in my mind: *If you charge him for me, the fact that we were married will condone his actions, but will anyone condone mine?*

Jodi surely didn't, and a moment later, when Bill and his coiled hair slithered into the frame like a copper snake to start the next story, his stare sent venom through my veins. I knew what he was thinking: *It's okay, everyone. No crime here. He married her.*

A few weeks following the news report, I drew dark lines through the boxes on the March calendar and lifted the page to April to mark the date that my divorce attorney, Ida Fletcher,

had given me earlier that afternoon. The thought of it drawing nearer made me feel especially anxious, and I jumped as
the phone rang, accidentally flinging the pen to the spot on
the carpet where the computer tower had sat until the day
the sheriff's office confiscated it in 2006. I quickly scooped up
the pen and leaned over to read the caller ID. My heart hurt
as I saw the words *Blocked Caller*.

"Hey," I said into the phone before Gary Richard could
say a word. "I spoke with my attorney today. I told her you
were planning on pleading guilty at your hearing in April. Is
that still correct?"

Gary Richard drew a long breath. "Yes. If I plead guilty
to the charge for you and the one soon to come in Lubbock
County, they're offering a plea deal."

I massaged the back of my neck, trying to keep the ten-
sion from rising. "What are they offering?"

"If I plead guilty for both counts of statutory rape, they
will run my sentences concurrently." He gave a short mirth-
less laugh. "Which means at most I will serve maybe four
or five years total for both counts before I get released on
parole."

I tucked a strand of hair behind my ear, stroking it slowly
as my thoughts took off in one direction. One stroke. *Daniel
will be a teen.* One stroke. *Ember won't be a toddler.* One stroke.
You'll miss milestones, school assemblies, growth spurts. One
stroke. *Who will teach Daniel to shave his face?*

"When are you going to tell them?" he said, cutting into
my thoughts.

"I thought about doing it tonight, after dinner."

"Okay. But, Caroline, will you please tell them how much
I love them and that none of this is their fault? Tell them that
even behind bars, I am always here for them."

"I will. You're their father, and they will always love you."
I paused, hearing a faint sniffle. "Gary Richard, just because
we aren't going to be married doesn't mean I will keep them
away from you. I am not like *those* mothers. They still need
their dad, even if it's from a distance."

A few hours later, I peeked into the living room, where
Ember stood high on her toes, mirroring the toy ballerina cir-
cling in the center of our glass table. My spirits fell with every
rise of her body, knowing that all too soon, reality would col-
lide with the magical world she was in.

Would her innocence be lost forever? Would she ache
for another dance with her daddy, like the one in which his
hand swallowed hers as he spun her in the center of rain-
bow-swirled bubbles floating from his deejay equipment?
Would she even remember? Would sorrow forever close her
throat when people asked where her daddy was? Would it
close my throat when she asked me?

Dabbing tears from my eyes, I inched closer to her. "Oh,
my beautiful princess, that is so pretty. You are such a good
dancer."

Shoving the hair away from her face, she grinned, then
her movements grew bigger and bigger as she danced for me.

I reached out my hand. "Let's go see what your brother is
doing."

We walked into Daniel's room, where we found him playing a video game.

"Hey, buddy, what are you doing?"

Without missing a beat, Daniel's fingers rapidly pressed
the buttons on the controller. "Playing *Star Wars*."

Ember ran into the clubhouse under his bed and grabbed
the controller dangling from the ledge.

"Move, Ember! I can't see!"

"Hey, sweetie, can you pause the game for a second? I need to talk to you and your sister."

His shoulders slumped. "Okay," he said, though he still pressed the buttons.

"I just need to talk to you for a minute, and then you can play a little longer."

I crawled into the clubhouse and pulled Ember with the controller onto my lap while Daniel scooted upright on the blue beanbag brushing my right leg.

"You know how much Daddy and I love you both, right?"

Daniel nodded, glancing back at the screen to make sure the characters hadn't moved.

"You know how some of the kids you go to school with have a mom and a dad, but they live in different houses because they are divorced?"

He tipped his head to the side.

"Your daddy and I love you both so much. Your daddy is a good daddy, but sometimes daddies and mommies do better if they aren't together. Daddy and I think we do better when we aren't together, but we still are your mommy and daddy. So even if we aren't together, we both are still here for you. Like you know how Daddy calls and talks to you from jail sometimes? Even though you can't see him, he is still here for you."

Daniel stopped looking at me and peered at Ember, who leaned forward, trying to reach the controller lying in his lap. He clutched it tighter, then tilted his head quizzically back at me.

I silently drew a breath, not breaking my gaze. I knew I needed to shorten my words so I didn't make this whole conversation bigger and scarier than it needed to be. Their worlds were going to change, but they also already had. They hadn't seen their dad in three months.

I corralled Ember back inside my arms. "Daniel, your daddy and I . . ." I reached out my hand to clasp his. "Your daddy and I are getting divorced."

Sadness clouded his features.

I wrapped my arm around him, sandwiching Ember between us. "I know that sounds like a scary word, but that just means your daddy and I won't be married any-more. So when Daddy gets out of jail, he will have another house."

Excitedly I gave him a wide smile. "You know what that means for you and your sister?"

Daniel rubbed his eyes. "What?"

"When Daddy gets a house, you and Ember will get to decorate your rooms any way you want. What color room would you like?"

His eyes shot sparks of intrigue at me. "Um, blue. Will Daddy let me have an Xbox too?"

"Of course he will."

Daniel danced in place, now happy, as Ember jumped up and tried to grab the controller again.

I grabbed her hand. "Daniel, you can play for about fif-teen more minutes, then you need to get ready for bed." I kissed his forehead, then scooped Ember into my arms, run-ning my fingers through her wispy blond hair.

We made our way toward her room to pick out pajamas for bed.

"Mommy loves you. Do you love Mommy?"

"Yes."

"How much do you love Mommy?"

She opened her arms wide. "Much." Then she pressed her hands to my cheeks.

Tears filled my eyes as I thought about the aftermath of this conversation and the devastation it would bring. I pictured the pillows saturated with tears as they cried themselves to sleep. Me trying to explain the *whys*.

But the whys didn't come. The kids seemed okay, and the whole thing seemed much more emotional for me. Maybe they didn't understand what I said. Perhaps they didn't know any questions to ask. Either way, I felt peace that, for the moment, their innocence wasn't lost. But it was mixed with fear for the day they would have questions I'd struggle to answer, and gratitude that this night I would get to decompress as I lay on my tear-stained pillow.

A few weeks later, perched in the wooden box next to the judge, I let my gaze follow the sunlight streaming from the glass to the history etched in the ceiling, thinking of all the times I had been here, in this courthouse, without seeing it from this view. I had always been in the row of chairs where my mom was sitting—the row behind Gary Richard. But for the first time in ten years, I was facing him, tracing with my eyes the block letters spelling out the word *jail* stamped across his orange jumpsuit. He stared at me, then glanced at the deputies who escorted him over to the courthouse that morning, then stared back at me.

I wonder if he's thinking what I am?

How did we get here?

According to the divorce papers, our marriage couldn't be preserved; it was irretrievably broken.

How did I get here?

The judge asked me to come next to him so he could ask me a few questions.

"Mrs. Downey."

The heaviness of the judge's voice pulled my eyes to him.

"Mrs. Downey, it says here that you are requesting to share custody with Mr. Downey and adhere to a standard visitation schedule. Do you feel that is in the best interest of your children?"

I stared past him, ignoring the condemnation in his tone. Catching sight of the specks of dust floating like the white fluff of a dandelion inside the streams of sunlight, I wondered if I blew a puff of air, could I make a wish and make it all go away? If maybe this was all just a dream. It wasn't, but I did make a wish; I wished that I could see God through the dark, that I could be something if I weren't a wife, that I could be a suitable mother. A wish that the humiliation would stop burning within.

I knew he didn't agree that a standard visitation schedule was in their best interest, but neither did Ida. Over these past few months, she and I had spoken about many things as we prepared the divorce papers. Due to our bankruptcy, we didn't have any marital property or debts to divide. Since Gary Richard and I weren't married when we had Daniel, the court required the filing of a parent-child relationship to legally establish a record with them indicating Gary Richard was his father.

When it came to the visitation schedule, I knew Gary Richard was going to prison, which would void any plan for a few years.

Ida had asked if I was sure, and I was, because that was as far as I could think. The best interest for me was to be divorced. I knew Gary Richard could delay it by refusing to sign, so Ida and I agreed to request the divorce standard: joint legal custody with physical custody granted to the mother.

Father gets every other weekend, one night during the week, rotating holidays, and one week in the summer. That way, Gary Richard would have nothing to reject.

"Mrs. Downey, you are aware of the charges that Mr. Downey is planning to plead guilty to, correct?"

I wanted to vomit. "I know, but he is their dad. I don't know the best thing to do, because they still love him."

"Thank you. You can go ahead and step down now."

I bit my bottom lip as I rounded the wooden banisters and inched closer to Gary Richard. He raised his cuffed hands, struggling to wipe the tears slipping down his cheeks. I looked at my mom's puckered lips; she was making the same face she made while she bandaged my scraped knee when I was a little girl. She felt my pain and his. I slid into the chair next to Ida at the wooden table, about two feet from Gary Richard.

We sat in silence, waiting as the judge riffled through the stack of fifteen papers containing nine years of marriage, all neatly packaged inside a beige folder. Then, raising his eyes over the top of his glasses, the judge looked at Gary Richard. "The request here is for standard visitation and custody. However, with your intent to plead guilty for statutory rape, I can't in good faith grant that request."

Gary Richard lowered his head.

The judge's gaze turned toward me. "Mrs. Downey, I am granting you sole legal and physical custody of the children. Due to Mr. Downey's current incarceration, there will be no visitation schedule required, and I am permitting you to decide when it is reasonable and proper for Mr. Downey to have visitation with the children. It will be at your discretion."

I nodded.

The judge turned toward my attorney. "I read the request proposed by you and Mrs. Downey to suspend the child support payments of six hundred dollars a month until Mr. Downey is released from prison. I will reduce the amount Mr. Downey owes to three hundred dollars. However, I will not suspend the payments."

He turned back to Gary Richard. "Because while you're incarcerated, Mrs. Downey will be solely providing for the children, a task that will not be easy. She is providing their food, clothing, shelter, school expenses, and medical support. She is entitled to your support, so while you are away, the payments will accrue, and when you are released, you will pay the current and back support."

Ida leaned into me. "Man, he stuck it to him," she whispered. "I thought he would at least drop it to fifty dollars a month while he is in there."

It was my turn to lower my head. *Is this when I smile because of a massive sum of money accruing?* I wondered bitterly. *Or is this when I cry, knowing it's a debt he will never be able to pay?*

Hearing the sounds of his chains, I gave a half smile as Gary Richard shuffled by with a haunted look. I felt alone in a room full of people.

Can you spread hate when a marriage is alive and still wash it with love-shaped tears as it dies? Does it depend on the frame? A sex offender or a father. A victim or a wife. The best interest of kids or self. A fairy tale or a drama. A spectator or a player. Free or caught.

Can I still miss you or not?

CHAPTER 18

INFECTED

I stepped outside the visitor-processing center and faced the door to the next building on the prison grounds. Fear crawled up my throat as I scanned the September sky peeking between rolls of barbed wire.

Why did I come here? What did I need to see, or say, or hear from Gary Richard?

When I asked my parents if they would keep the kids over the weekend, I said I needed to make the five-hour drive to see if the prison was too scary to bring the kids to visit their dad, who hadn't seen them in nine months. I told myself I needed closure. To find a release, because five months after the divorce, pain continued to suffocate me like the chain-link tunnel I was now walking through.

Breathe, Caroline. Breathe, I silently told myself as the approaching door grew larger with every step. What was on the other side? I quickly found out.

More screenings like in the first building. They mimicked airport security minus the excitement of a vacation, a bag to carry on, or the freedom of a runway. Monotone guards commanded my every move and patted me down for contraband. Then they instructed that I leave my purse and keys in a locker. They brushed over my clothes with a wand to detect traces of drugs.

Didn't they know I wouldn't do that? Couldn't they tell by my eyebrow twitching that I was terrified? Couldn't they detect by my lips tucked tightly together that I was only trying to act brave? Because *brave* was what everyone kept telling me I was.

"You're so brave raising two young children on your own. So strong. How do you do it by yourself?" well-meaning family and friends asked over and over, as if I had an answer, as though I had a choice.

I'd always shrug and smile and respond that I didn't know how I was doing it; I just was.

I wasn't brave. I just didn't know where or when it was acceptable for a single woman, a single mother, to say or show she was scared, because if I admitted that, who would be there to hold my hand and tell me it was going to be okay?

My eyes shut tightly at the unwelcoming buzz of the door, and I told myself, *You can do this, Caroline. You can do this.*

Though I couldn't see the sign that read Visitors' Center, I could feel the guards behind the blackened windows and cameras that hung from every corner staring at me. I drew a breath, searching for a different moment in time when his prison sentence wouldn't feel like mine. Wondering if I squeezed my eyes tighter, could I get lost in another life, another world, like I had tried to do every weekend since our divorce? Then my thoughts transitioned to that Friday night a few weeks before when I made plans to do just that, when I'd invited my friend Joni to go out to a local bar to dance and get drunk. That had become our weekend ritual. Only, this particular weekend, she couldn't make it. Her parents were out of town, and she'd promised that she would check on their dogs.

While we were on the phone, Joni's mom called, so she put me on hold.

Disappointed, I pushed my head into the pile of unmatched socks and kid-sized T-shirts I was sorting on the floor. *Guess I'll have to figure out something for the kids and me to do. I'm sure they won't want to watch movies at home two nights in a row.*

"Hey, you still there?" Joni clicked back on the line, her voice sounding excited.

I sat up straight. "Yep."

"Mom said you should come down with me and help with the dogs. She said we could just spend the night, and then I wouldn't need to drive back down Sunday morning to let them out again. Do you wanna?" She paused, though not long enough for me to answer. "We could hit up Double Barrel first, then walk across the parking lot to The Blue Moon. It isn't like that club you always want to go to up north of your house, the one with the drag shows by that railroad crossing. What's their name again?"

"Neon Lights."

"Yeah, yeah. It isn't exactly like that, but I hear they play some pretty good dance music for a small town, plus some younger guys I went to high school with hang out around there. They're around your age. We can meet up with them, and I could introduce you."

My spirits lifted immediately. "I'm in! That sounds fun. Let me call our babysitter."

The next night, around nine thirty, the bouncer at The Blue Moon put a black checkmark across my hand after checking our IDs and taking our money.

"You don't look twenty-seven," he said as his eyes scanned the jeans tightly hugging my thighs. "I thought you were barely twenty-one."

My flesh tingled.

"Come on, let's go get a drink," I said, knotting my arm around Joni's elbow and pulling my eyes away from the anchor tattoo chiseled into his left bicep.

"Ian!" Joni threw her arms around the waist of a tall guy with inky black hair who was leaning his back into the bar. "Caroline, this is my friend Susie's baby brother, Ian."

Ian cocked his head, eyes only meeting my chest.

"It's nice to meet you," I shouted over the music.

Ian turned and motioned to the bartender.

I fiddled with my earring as my face grew hot. *Is he a jerk, or could he not hear me over the music?*

"What do you want to drink?" Ian said, pinning me with his eyes. Then, without taking his eyes off me, he slid his empty glass toward the back of the bar. "I'll buy you ladies something."

Over the next few hours, I lost track of time, drink count, conversations, and my inhibitions. On the dance floor, I was thrusting my backside into Ian as he picked sweat-saturated hair from my neck, percolating desire between us.

"What do you say we have an after-party when we leave here?" he breathed in my ear.

I turned around. Longing whispered through me.

Minutes later, Ian locked the door to the bedroom down the hall as laughter trailed after us from the living room, where Joni and three of Ian's friends were playing with the dogs. Ian crawled up my body as I stretched across the bed like an insect caught in silk.

I closed my eyes, waiting with anticipation as every inch of me ached with need. Desire weaved its web of seduction to nourish my need to be touched; to be wanted by someone who wasn't a child; to be seen as a woman, not a mother or another man's rejection; to be free. *Am I the prey? Predator? A jezebel? Wicked woman?*

At that moment, I didn't care.

Within seconds, his smoky breath penetrated my nostrils. Hints of sweet sugar and stale licorice from the whiskey and Coke he drank at the bar caused my breath to hitch. I was smelling that same foul smell that had flowed from my Papaw Clyde's mouth as he leaned in to kiss me goodbye while he touched me inappropriately and took my childhood innocence.

My eyes flew open, and I stared frantically into a velvet curtain of darkness. I was no longer craving this guy as I had been just moments before. Silently begging his body to stop crushing mine, I breathed a quiet sigh of relief when it did. Then he rolled his exhausted body off me, splattering me with beads of sweat.

"I'm sorry, I just need a minute to rest," Ian said, panting. "Sometimes when I've had too much to drink, it just doesn't work like . . ." His words ended with a soft snore.

I lay there stiff, naked, silent. But my mind was anything but silent.

What are you doing, Caroline? Who are you? Other than dirty. Gross. Unfit to be a mother or anybody else's wife. I see you—the girl with bedroom eyes, painted-on jeans, telling white lies. How quick are you going to call the doctor this time to ease your fear of getting an STD because you're too stupid to protect yourself? Oh, let us not forget how you like to rinse and repeat.

Faces of men I'd had flashed across my mind.

What's the body count since your divorce? Do you have enough hands? Who do you think you're fooling? You said this was the last time. And umm, when was that? Oh, yeah. Last weekend, after you slept with the guy you met on that dating site. You swore you wouldn't have sex with random men again. Remind me. What's Ian's last name?

Ian moved his arm.

Stop! Please stop. I'm sorry. I won't do it anymore.

I closed my eyes, trying to swallow a still-beating heart. *God, if You can hear me, please make this stop! I promise no more. I won't keep doing this. I need an escape from the life that feels too much to do on my own, but there has to be another way, because every time I return to this, I'm tangled in pain. I know I don't have the right to ask. I cursed at You. I was too angry, too naughty, too reckless for You to stay. I don't expect You to love me anymore, but, God, could You please come back, just for one night, because I'm scared of being alone.*

A grinding sound snapped my mind back to the present moment; it was coming from the metal locks on the door leading into the inmate visiting area.

"Sign in, please," the guard with the salt-and-pepper hair said while he pressed the rubber stamp into my hand like the bouncer at The Blue Moon.

On the counter, I placed the baggie full of change Gary Richard asked me to bring—for the vending machine—and then I signed my name for what seemed like the millionth time.

For months I had been signing my name to try and see him. I signed it on the visitor application to be approved to visit. After getting denied because the restraining order against him was still active, I signed it again. And I signed once again to appeal another denial, made because I was one of the victims of his sex crimes. I understood why they denied a perpetrator's request to add his victim to his visiting list. Yet every time I had to explain the situation again, I sighed with resentment, knowing that *other* mothers, *normal* mothers, didn't have to go through all this red tape to take their young children to visit their father.

The guard unlocked the wire-mesh door, and my eyes gravitated from the concrete floor to the bars of fluorescent lighting hanging from the ceiling. The room was open and bright, a perplexing yet refreshing surprise because it was exactly the opposite of the dark dungeon I had painted in my mind's eye. I zigzagged between the stack of used board games, the crayons in the buckets, and the cartoon mural spanning the length of the wall accented by other cartoons flashing on the television in the area designated for children. This wasn't scary. This felt normal, safe.

Seconds later, I slid into one of four empty chairs and watched the door that the guard told me Gary Richard would come through. I folded my hands in my lap, then transferred them to the table, where I drummed my fingers. I waited. I shifted my body as I surveyed the selection of chips, candy bars, and other snacks in the vending machines. Then something interesting caught my eye. I stared at a man fighting back tears as he stood to take a photo between a solemn-faced little boy and an older woman whose silver-streaked hair captivated me. I wondered what their story was.

What words did that little boy say to his daddy, if that was his daddy? What words did his daddy, her son, say to them? My eyes zoomed out on the endless people around the room, and I wondered about each of their stories. What was so funny at the table where the man with the dimpled chin gave the man sitting next to him a belly-sized laugh? Did the woman at the table next to me want to passionately kiss the lips of the man who looked twenty years younger? Why did the man with untamed hair have to stay behind the glass as he stared into the eyes of the woman he was talking to through a phone receiver? What story was the little girl with curly hair excitedly telling as her prisoner father looked at her with the same eyes my kids have on Christmas morning?

I looked at the door again. Part of me was ready to see Gary Richard walk through it, and the other part wasn't. What expressions would I make when I saw him? What expression would he make when he saw me? The hawk-eyed guard, perched roughly ten feet from the door, started to move toward it. I brushed my hands along my thighs, hoping to calm the nerves racing through my body, but when I saw Gary Richard's profile fill the portrait-sized window, I stopped.

As he walked toward me, everybody and everything else fell off the horizon of Gary Richard's presence, and I thought how good that white T-shirt looked against his golden skin and under those prison grays. His smile slipped out as it did that day I walked toward him in his bedroom when I was sixteen. Warmth spread through me.

The closer he got, the more I began debating how I was supposed to greet him. The prison rules stated that prisoners were allowed only one greeting and one departing embrace—either a hug and/or a kiss. Gary Richard hadn't had a touch from me in nine months. Wouldn't it be kind to give that to him? Wouldn't that let him know, as my children's father, that I cared for him?

Do I hug him? Clutch his hand? Or should I just smile? I had no desire to kiss him, at least not in front of the guards spaced throughout the room. But my heart was thumping wildly. Maybe because of the passionate history held in his plump lips or the unwavering confidence in his shoulders. It was clear his presence turned me on, but where was the switch to turn it off?

Why did it feel as though he still had the controls?

He tilted his head back and smirked at a couple of inmates sitting adjacent to me. I watched with awe as my favorite man put on his regular show, even after so much of him had been exposed. I couldn't let go.

Over the past five months, flames of anger had shot through me as friends of his, and some of mine, admitted to things they knew about him but didn't confess to me until he had gone to prison. I heard about more adulterous acts. I heard how he manipulated me by flattening my tire at work, demagnetizing my bank card before I went shopping with my mom and sister, and tampering with our furnace so it wouldn't turn on. I learned about him mixing metal shavings in my motor oil, causing the engine to seize the day I took Daniel to weightlifting practice. So many lies; so much unsafe, dangerous, toxic behavior all to control me, to make me call him for help so I would see how much I needed him and change my mind about our divorce.

Since he'd been in prison, he'd call occasionally, and I would confront him about what I had heard. He would deny it all on the spot, then admit to some of it weeks later, either over the phone or in a letter. His lines were always the same: He was sorry, and he didn't want to lose me. He had acted out because he didn't know what else to do. He had no choice, because I had ruined his life the day I gave my statement to the sheriff. He never touched any of the other girls, only me. He had pleaded guilty to the one in Lubbock County only because they agreed to run the sentences together if he did. The prosecutor knew the evidence on all the others was weak. The only people I should be mad at were her and Frank, because they used me as bait so they could use the one thing he couldn't deny—his son's DNA.

It was lies, all of it. Of course it was. And I knew it. So how was it possible that I was now greeting him happily and feeling that tingling feeling again? How was it possible that as I breathlessly stared down my enemy, all traces of rage extinguished? That I could look into his sparkling eyes with desire and feel pleased that he was sliding into the chair next to me? While smiling?!

"Hey, I was starting to get worried that something happened to you," Gary Richard said, smiling at the bag of quarters that lay in front of him on the table. "Visiting hours are over at six thirty."

The clock above the coffee pot read 4:55 p.m.

"Yeah, I know I'm later than I said I would be. Sorry, the drive took a little longer than I thought, and—" I exhaled, raising my eyes toward the ceiling. "And, well, this whole screening process of getting in here takes a while."

"Thanks for bringing these." He raised a fistful of change. "I feel like I haven't had anything good in here. I told Daniel that I was missing the Blizzards from Dairy Queen!"

I tried to smile, but I'm sure it came across as a smirk, because I was so irritated, remembering. I had heard him say that to Daniel on one of his phone calls to the kids. When he called, I'd hand Daniel or Ember the phone and watch as a wide-eyed Daniel told his dad about his new video games and as Ember pushed her doll up to the phone to "show" her daddy, her face shining brightly. I stood by, too, when sadness clouded Daniel's features as his daddy told him the prison was cold. And I pulled Daniel into my arms when he hung up and asked if we could send his daddy one of his blankets. I stayed by their sides when Ember's smile faded as he told her, "I'm gonna get that chicken belly," and she realized that the only one who could reach out and tickle her stomach was me.

"Yeah, he told me that," I said. "We do need to talk about that."

Gary Richard leaned back in the chair.

"When you call and talk about things you miss or don't have because you're in here, it makes them sad. They worry about you." I was surprised when tears appeared in my eyes.

Gary Richard sat up, moving the quarters into each hand like a slinky.

"Like the time you told Daniel you were cold," I pushed on, letting out an exasperated sigh. "Gary Richard, he asked me how he could send you one of his blankets."

Gary Richard dropped his head for what seemed like minutes. "He is such a sweet boy to want to take care of his dad like that." Then he slid back into his chair. "Do you want anything from the machine?"

I paused and blinked. "Just a bottle of water."

Gary Richard returned, tossing down nacho-flavored chips, water, and peanuts covered in chocolate. "You can have some if you want."

"Thanks." I popped a couple of peanuts into my mouth. "I want to bring the kids to see you. But before I do, I think it's a good idea for you and me to talk about us and where we stand."

"Okay, Caroline, whatever it takes. I just want to see the kids and stay active in their lives while I'm in here."

"I want that too. I don't want to be one of those parents who use the kids as a weapon when we aren't getting along. We aren't ever getting back together, but we will always be their parents and need to do what's best for them. There isn't a manual for how this is all supposed to work, how you co-parent behind bars."

"It would help if you would bring them to see me," Gary Richard said, crinkling the bag of chips.

"I am not trying to keep them from you," I said, frowning. "As I told you on the phone, I wanted to check it out first, because I don't want to scare them by bringing them into a place like this. But it isn't all that scary, and I know Ember will want to play that fishing game over there with you." I pointed to the blue box on the table by the children's area.

His mouth curled up into a fond smile. "I'd really like that."

"I'll probably bring them down in a few weeks or so. I know they'll be excited to swim at the hotel."

"I can't believe there are only ten minutes left." He propped his chin on his hand. "How are your parents doing?" Before I could say anything, he cocked his head toward me and put on a crooked smile. "How many guys have you been on dates with since I've been gone?"

Heat crawled up my cheeks.

Why did I come here? I couldn't respond to that question. I couldn't explain why I didn't have an answer or a number.

Did one-night stands count as dates? What about the men who asked, but I said no because their friendliness was uncomfortable? Scary?

I glanced toward the guard with his thumbs tucked in his belt, wishing he would announce that any second I was going to need to leave because visiting hours were over. "I am not dating right now. Too busy with the kids."

It was a lie, but a lie laced with some truth. I *was* busy with the kids. I wasn't really *dating* anyone. And after Ian, I had promised God no more one-night stands.

But Gary Richard didn't know. He didn't know about my unsafe behaviors, though they mirrored his. He didn't know how many times I paid a sitter to keep his kids while I headed out to party and get drunk. He didn't know how confused my mind was as I swirled out into uncharted seas, trying to find myself while aching to be seen by others. He didn't know how addicted to toxic behavior I had become after years of it spreading through my veins.

Following the rules of a departing embrace, I hugged him long enough to hear him inhale the white-grapefruit-and-mint shampoo scent in my hair. "I'll bring the kids down soon."

"Okay. Thank you for coming. Drive safe," he said, breathing in my ear.

Longing whispered through me.

As I got into the car and made my way to the hotel, I thought about how intertwined our lives still seemed. I wondered if he felt as lost as I did as he made his way back to his cell. Was I a fool? Or still in love? Or too afraid to let him go?

He blamed me, but I also blamed him for leaving me alone with our kids. For the consequences we had to face, though they should have been his to pay. Did he cry out to God, as I had done so many nights, asking to be protected? Did he feel unseen, like society had rejected him? Did his insides feel corroded with guilt, remorse, and shame? Were we really one and the same?

They called him a predator, but did he, too, feel like prey? Or was I the only one wondering how to keep the shadows in my mind at bay? If I no longer used the mattress to try and penetrate my pain, was there another way? Or would fear always be a knot in my stomach, leaving me unsure how to function, a splinter in my heart, convincing me I would never find love again because of my past, my thoughts?

I kept my eyes on the road as my thoughts whizzed by as quickly as the road signs. But one thought stuck with me: *Can I move on with my life—or are my wounds too infected?*

CHAPTER 19

THE RULES

"You ready to see Daddy?"

Ember's pigtails bounced as she bobbed her head. "Uh-huh."

We were seated in the prison's visitors' room, waiting for her and Daniel's first visit with Gary Richard. "Now remember what Mommy told you in the car. When Daddy comes out, you have to stay in your chair like a big girl."

She nodded, then wiggled up onto her knees.

"Which game do you want to play with Daddy?" I pointed to the stacks of games in the children's area; nothing had moved since I'd visited the prison in September, and it was the beginning of November.

Recognition dawned on her face. "Fishies!"

A smile danced on my lips. "I told you they had the fishing game here." I turned my attention to ten-year-old Daniel, who had his eyes locked on a tattered box on the top shelf. "And what about you?"

"I was thinking. I'm going to ask Dad if we can play dominoes and do that puzzle."

"Awesome! That will be fun. I know Daddy is so excited to see both of you."

I glanced at each of them as we waited expectantly for Gary Richard to come down from his cell. I wondered if I'd done enough to prepare them for this visit. In the 350 miles we had driven to get here, I had excitedly told them about the guards, the screenings, and the barbed wire, as though we were embarking on a new adventure. I had prepared to answer questions when I told them Daddy couldn't hold them on his lap—because those were the rules. But the questions never came. Instead I saw joy fill their eyes like sunshine as I told them they would get to swim in the hotel pool and buy things from the vending machines with their baggie full of quarters. I saw that joy again the following day when I told them how nice they looked, as I tucked Ember's shirt into her pastel camo-print pants and smoothed down the neckline of Daniel's shirt in the prison's parking lot.

Now sitting here, knowing in minutes they would see their dad for the first time in eleven months, I scanned. I scanned the door framed by the guard, where I saw Gary Richard's profile fill the window. I scanned Daniel's and Ember's faces, looking for twitches of worry, short breaths, tears of distress, or signs that they saw him too. I chased their reactions like butterflies, holding them in my gaze, trying not to crush the moment with one ounce of fear, confusion, sadness, or pain.

"Look who I see!" I lilted my voice as if I were singing them a nursery rhyme. I smiled brightly.

Their heads swiveled in sync toward the door. "Daddy!"

Instantly, Ember's splayed fingers covered her eyes with one hand while Daniel's eyebrows rose high above his glasses. Gary Richard's eyes twinkled as he darted across the room, opening his arms wide, triggering Daniel to explode out of the chair. Gary Richard hugged him for only seconds—because those were the rules. Then he brushed my shoulder with his as I stood, clutching Ember's hand. He lowered down enough to allow her arms to fling around his neck and hugged her for only seconds—because those were the rules.

"Hold me, Daddy. Hold me," Ember whimpered, stretching her arms in the air.

With tears in his eyes, Gary Richard stepped back, looked up to the ceiling, and blinked hard. "I can't, sweetie, I can't."

I held her hand lightly and pulled her gently back toward her chair. "Remember what Mommy said in the car? Daddy can't hold you, baby. Let's sit back down." I pointed toward the chair between Daniel and Ember. "Daddy will sit in that one so he will be right by you."

Moments later, while staring endlessly at the kids, Gary Richard placed his palms on the table. "It's so good to see you both."

I knew he would rather kiss their faces, or stroke their hair, or hold them tightly inside his arms when he told them that, but he couldn't—because those were the rules. I knew he would rather chase them around outside, surrounded by their laughter, than walk alone to pick up the first game for them to play, surrounded by their silence, but he couldn't—because those were the rules. I knew they would rather be sprawled across the carpet knocking over dominoes as they jumped on Gary Richard's back to wrestle instead of sitting upright in these stiff chairs. Still, they couldn't—because those were the rules of the prisoner and the children; it was the sentence we all shared.

"Everything go all right getting in here?" Gary Richard asked, tapping the dominoes on the table.

I lifted my shoulder in a half shrug. "Yeah, but I did have to change Ember's pants. They were camo print, and the rules say you can't wear camouflage into the prison; I saw it was listed as prohibited under the rules for the dress code but thought it meant the dark green like those military jackets."

"Well, that's ridiculous. She's a little girl. What does it matter?"

"No clue. That's kind of what I thought, but those are the rules." I sneered. "Hers were baby blue, tan, and gray, but the guards up front said it didn't matter because it was still a camo print. Luckily"—I paused, looking down at Ember's jeans—"since we checked out of the hotel this morning, we have our suitcases in the trunk of the rental car, so I had something to change her into."

Gary Richard let out a harsh breath as he scooped some quarters out of the baggie. "I'll go get us some drinks and snacks." He offered both the kids a grin as he walked away.

I leaned into Daniel. "Did you tell your dad about the signs you made when you ran for student council?"

"Dad!" Daniel's face lit up as Gary Richard slid cans of pop in front of us.

"Hold on, buddy. I'll be right back." Jingling the coins, he headed toward the machine that had the same selection of chips and candies I had seen a few months ago.

"Dad. Me and Mom made these posters when I ran for student council. They were so cool. We glued a picture of a fan on them, and they said *Be a fan, vote for Dan*. I hung them in the hall, and all the kids said they were really cool."

"Those sound like they were cool." Gary Richard chuckled. "So cool you won. I'm proud of you, buddy! You're such a good student and a great leader for your fifth-grade class.

Your mom also told me you're still getting straight As. You're smart—you must get that from me." He flashed a half smile and a wink in my direction.

I slipped Gary Richard a curious glance. "He is so smart, and I am proud of him too." I watched Daniel offer a toothy smile. Hearing Ember crunching on a cracker, I turned toward her. "And, Miss Ember, tell Daddy about your birthday."

Gary Richard leaned her direction. "Can't believe Daddy's little girl is four now."

Ember's eyes crinkled as she pushed the rest of the cracker in her mouth.

"What did you do for your birthday?" he asked, pretending I hadn't already told him on one of our phone conversations.

"We went to the park," she mumbled, with her mouth still full. "It was so windy all my balloons blew away." Then she folded her arms in frustration, catching us all off guard and causing laughter to spread around the table.

This was family time, ours. This was the time we all needed with the dad I wanted him to be. The one they needed him to be. One who was present and focused. Not the kind of dad I scolded when weeks would go by without a phone call or letter. Not the type of dad I'd rant about when he would shift the focus of his letters or calls to me, pleading for us to get back together. Not the sort of man who made remarks about how my struggles were nothing compared to his. We needed *this* guy, the kind of dad who was engaging and consistent. And for two hours, I watched as he was all of that.

He talked with Daniel about baseball, giving him tips and reminding him that just because Dad was no longer his coach didn't mean he didn't need to practice catch at home.

He talked to Ember about dance class and day care, reminding her that she needed to listen to her teachers and share her toys with her friends. He told them they needed to listen to Mommy and to help out around the house. He grinned at me when Daniel didn't take a breath telling him about scientific facts he'd learned in class, and when Ember aggravated Daniel by not giving him the piece of the puzzle he needed. He pursed his lips when Ember started grabbing the fish with her hand because her magnetic pole wasn't scooping them up as quickly as his. And although those weren't the rules, no way was she losing to her daddy.

As families and inmates slowly began to disappear throughout the room, we knew visiting hours were winding down.

"Too bad you couldn't have stayed another night. It's gonna be late by the time you get home," Gary Richard stated as we walked toward the foggy gray backdrop, the same one I had seen the solemn-faced little boy stand in front of with the man I assumed was his dad the first time I was here.

I sighed. "Yeah, that would have been nice. But it's okay. I can't afford that right now with the repairs I am doing to get the place we are going to rent from my sister ready for us to move into in the next few months."

"You can go ahead and step in for your picture," the inmate assigned to work in the visitors' area told us.

I stood next to the camera and watched as Gary Richard wrapped his arm around Daniel, who stood expressionless at his left side, while holding Ember, who awkwardly angled her head toward Gary Richard's shoulder as if she wanted to lay on it but wasn't sure if she could. Watching this scene reminded me of a conversation about photos I'd had with a counselor for the first and last time seven months prior.

"Before we bring your son in, what brings you here to see me?" The counselor's voice was angelic, like his winter-white hair.

I exhaled. "Recently, I've gotten a divorce, and I don't know how to help my kids. I don't want to mess them up for life. I try to ask people what they think I should do, and they just say I should talk to someone." I shrugged. "So here I am. There is nothing really wrong. My son seems to be doing okay, and my daughter is only three, so she doesn't really understand. But I brought Daniel here hoping you could talk to him, make sure he really is doing okay. I just don't want to miss something." My lips started to tremble.

The counselor's time-worn hands handed me a box of tissues, and we sat silent as I dabbed my eyes. There was wisdom in the space he gave me; it strengthened my voice to speak again.

"I am scared to take the family photos off the wall because I don't want to hurt my kids. After all, he is still their dad, but how do I keep things the same for them when everything has changed?"

"I don't know that you do. Things *have* changed. The family photo has changed. The environment of the home is now different; his things are no longer there. They see that, and that's okay that they do. One way to help with the transition, as you begin removing the family photos from the living room walls, is to give each child a picture of their dad to display in their room. That's a great way to communicate that although the environment inside the home has changed, they can still recognize he is their father, and they get to display his photos in their rooms any way they choose."

"That's a good idea; I can do that."

"I will meet with your son, but it sounds like he is doing okay. Kids need security, a place to feel safe, supported, loved. Sometimes as parents, when we feel an emotion, we assume that our kids must be feeling that too. We tell ourselves a story about how we believe they are feeling based on how we are. Can I ask if you have a particular belief? Do you believe in God?"

I could feel the heat of conviction stain my cheeks. I hadn't been to church regularly since before my divorce and had questioned God's existence many times. "Yes," I admitted. "I believe in God."

"What do you see when you talk to God? Do you see a face? A light?"

The photographer's shrill pitch burst through the memory, and I saw Gary Richard smiling larger than the kids. "This is gonna be a great picture."

I nodded, although he was speaking into the chilly prison air. I wondered if Daniel would put this photo next to the one of him and his dad wearing matching Royals gear from their first baseball game together that sat on his dresser. I wondered if Ember would put it next to the one of her and her daddy making silly faces inside a shark jaw from our beach vacation that sat next to her television.

A short while later, Gary Richard gave us all a departing embrace. I sensed his legs getting heavier with every step as he walked away from us. "Please come back to see me soon, okay?"

I looked down and away, unsure who should answer. And if it was me, I wasn't sure what I would say. What were the rules for this? The counselor said my job was to make my children feel safe, and the judge said I was to decide what was in the children's best interest. So what was I to do? My heart said seeing him was in their best interest, but now it ached and had no clue. Because as they hugged their daddy goodbye, they squeezed their eyes tight, needing shelter from their pain, like two butterflies hiding from the rain.

CHAPTER 20

MORE LIKELY

I clutched the empty shelf, silently standing in a strip of light coming from Ember's window, hearing Mom's voice echo from the garage across the barren kitchen.

"Caroline, the kids rode with your dad to unpack the truck. Anything else in here for us to load up?" She paused, then her voice grew louder. "Caroline!"

I wanted to shout, "I'm here. I just have one more box to load." But my throat had thickened with sobs, as I realized I couldn't pack the sweet musky air infused with vanilla Play-Doh and floral-scented dryer sheets, which was the only thing left inside the closet between the kids' rooms.

"Hon, where are you?" Her voice was strong, then faded like waves breaking along the shore. Although I couldn't see her face, I knew worry had washed over it.

Silently staggering, I bumped against Ember's door, falling into my mother's arms as she rounded the corner.

"Oh, honey."

"I don't know why I'm crying like this, but it—it hurts, Mom. It hurts so bad."

"Oh, sweetie, I am sorry. I know this is hard on you and the kids." Her voice cracked. "If I could, I would take all this pain from you."

"I shouldn't have gone back in there. I was handling it all okay, and then . . . then . . . that smell, oh, Mom, that smell." I coughed between stuttered breaths, trying to clear my throat. "I can't do this. I can't leave that smell, this kitchen, my flowers . . . they haven't even bloomed."

She rocked me from side to side, hypnotically. Her words, "Oooh, baby, it's gonna be okay," seamlessly transitioned into a hum. Every sway was meant to soothe; every tone was meant to remind me I wasn't alone. But comfort wouldn't come. It couldn't because the little girl inside my body was a vacant shell, a victim of the burned-out life Gary Richard and I had built together. I was left alone to sift through the memory-ashes of our home.

I thought of the parties we had hosted, filled with music and laughter. I thought of the day we'd brought our baby girl home from the hospital, vowing to keep her safe, just like Daniel had promised the baby squirrel he found outside in the tree. I thought of the voices raised in anger and betrayal and about the night that ended with shattered glass and hate. I thought of the glare from the computer monitor, weeks after the kids and I visited Gary Richard in prison, as I read articles telling me that statistically, my children were more likely to end up there. I thought of the ill words spoken under my breath as I bundled another stack of foreclosure notices and tucked them next to the Chapter 7 bankruptcy papers in the filing cabinet in our office.

I pulled away from my mom. "It just isn't fair! Why do I always have to be the one who struggles? Why is my life cursed?"

"Honey, it's not. You are just hurt right now. You've been through a lot, I don't know why, but I know you believe in

God, and you have to have faith it will get better. Your dad, sister, and I all say how strong you are all the time and how lucky the kids are to have you as their mom."

"Yeah! Real lucky." I let out an exasperated sigh. "A mom who can't afford to keep a roof over their heads. I can't support us on ten dollars an hour. The bankruptcy attorney certainly agreed when he offered to pray for me." I rolled my eyes at the empty counters. "If it weren't for you and Dad scraping together money for the down payment for Blair and Clay to buy the house for me to rent, where would the kids and I be?"

I paused, not long enough for a response but for comprehension to dawn on her face.

"Homeless?" I gave a half shrug. "Guess those single-parent-home, teenage-mom, doomed-to-a-life-of-poverty stats are accurate after all."

"Oh, Caroline." She tittered at my attempt to put my life in perspective, then dabbed the corners of her eyes. "Stop! It won't always feel like this, you know. We are here for you, and we will do all we can to help you in any way. That is what families are for. We help each other, that's what we do."

I lowered my head. "But why am I always the one who needs help? You all have spent five months turning a one-bedroom house into three so I can rent something I can afford. I can't ever repay you for that. I'm almost thirty, and I have nothing. No home! No savings! Credit that's shot. I've tried to have hope, but reality reminds me pretty quickly I shouldn't."

Mom folded her arms and looked down at the Berber carpet.

"Look around, Mom, look around! I can't have the life of my dreams because I chose the wrong man at sixteen! And here you are still helping your rebellious teen. Aren't you sick of helping me? Don't you feel like I should be helping you?"

"No, Caroline. No." She pressed her palm against my cheek. "We don't help each other to be paid back, and we don't keep a tally. We do what we can to help because we love you. I love you. I am your mother, and helping you is what I am here to do."

"But don't you ever get tired of helping everyone else? You have four grown kids, and I am already so exhausted with an eleven- and four-year-old. You had Dad to help. I don't know how I will ever be able to do all this alone."

Bitterness filled my mouth. "Mom, I want to believe my life can change for the better, but I have watched you and Dad spend your whole lives helping everyone, all the time. Why don't you, of all people, have more than you have?"

She didn't respond.

I drew a long breath. I didn't mean to hurt her, but I did. I knew I had to move on, face the unknowns, change with the seasons. *But how do I get springs of hope to flow with the river of my dreams frozen?*

Pinning my eyes to hers, I sighed softly. "I have watched Dad's body break down over years of trying to keep food on our table. I watched you never sit down as you served us your whole life. I've watched Dad's brain, back, and heart surgeries cripple your finances and chain you to a debt you'll never be able to repay. So how fair is this life, Mom? Can things really change? Can they?"

She let out a harsh breath. "Caroline!" She hollered my name like she did my dad's when he needed to calm down. And like him, I didn't.

"You know what the statistics say? They say my children are more likely to wear guilt, embarrassment, and shame because of the stigmas that come with their daddy's prison grays," I said, remembering the hundreds of articles I'd read. "How do I make them feel they belong in a world when every message screams they don't? Or is it like the statistics say: once you're in the cycle of poverty and crimes, it's more likely to keep repeating, so why try? So please, tell me how my life will ever be fine."

She nodded slowly, stepping back to open a cabinet door. "Well, it isn't fine that you don't have all these cabinets in the new house."

I made a *tsk* sound. "Mom."

"What?" she said and chuckled lightly. "I'm just saying I always loved this kitchen."

"Me too." I reached forward, brushing the countertop with my hand. "I'm sorry about what I said. Life just isn't fair sometimes."

Her fingers raked through the layers of my hair, every strand falling like the golden-yellow leaves of autumn. "I know, baby. I know."

I wanted to stay inside her arms forever, to fall back to the time when all I had to do was just be, with no responsibilities except coming inside for supper when she hollered my name.

"We should probably finish up here. You know your dad will be wondering what's taking us so long. Is there anything else to load up in here?"

"No."

"What are you doing with those blue totes in the garage that are duct-taped?"

I blew out my cheeks. "Those are what's left of Gary Richard's things. I guess we will need to load those up."

"Oh! I thought you said you weren't taking any of his stuff. You know what you said about new beginnings and all?"

I massaged the back of my neck. "I know. I don't want to because I don't have the extra space, but I don't know what else to do. He said he didn't have anyone else to store them for him until his brother gets out of prison, so he begged me to hang on to them until then. I told him that wasn't my problem, then felt bad because I know he doesn't have anyone else. So I told him I would put them in the shed for now."

We slowly walked out of the house while I tried to keep my tears from flooding out. This was the last time I would be in this house. I had to let it go and look forward to a new beginning—a beginning filled with more unknowns than I could count.

A short drive later, Mom and I made our way up to the new house, where we joined in with my dad, sister, and kids unloading and unpacking six and a half years' worth of items that filled 1,152 square feet, condensed and stacked against every wall of the 728 we would now occupy.

Determined to get it all unpacked, we ordered pizza for supper, took a quick break, and got back to work.

Later that night, after everyone went home, I carried a sleeping Ember from the couch to her new bedroom and tucked her in. Then I found Daniel asleep in his room, lying on top of his comforter and still holding the controller to his video game as if he were playing in his sleep. I jostled his shoulder. "Daniel, here, let me help you get under the cover."

His eyes opened slightly, but he was so tired he barely moved as I tugged at the comforter. Finally, I let him be and pressed my lips into his forehead. "Thank you for helping today."

After turning out his light, I wandered past the boxes with picture frames and decorative signs sitting next to the arched doorway, making a mental note that I would hang those up in the morning. Letting out a sigh, I fell on top of my bed and rubbed my neck as I thought about all the work I still had to do. I stiffened at the sounds of the water heater popping, so unfamiliar in this new place. I had a lot of new sounds and shadows to get used to. My eyes darted around the room, making sure the sounds and shadows were not a threat. I was just so tired—from the day's work, but also from the stress of the move and so many changes in our lives. My eyelids grew heavy, and I rolled over, hoping that we would settle in quickly and feel safe and happy here, that this would truly feel like home to us. I tucked the edges of the blanket under me, then blew out a series of short breaths before I fell asleep. We were really on our own now.

The following weekend, the kids and I spent Easter dipping boiled eggs into colored water, just as we had done every year, carrying an old tradition into a "new" home (that was fifty years older than me). I hoped the familiar ritual would bring them comfort. Earlier I'd pasted inspirational words—*Learn from Yesterday. Live for Today. Hope for Tomorrow*—on a weathered wall. Now I hoped those words would inspire them to smile, to dream, and to feel that they could rise above the what-ifs, the pity, the sins of their father, the statistics.

Several weeks later, in May 2008, I sat at half-court on the gym floor for the awards assembly at Daniel's elementary school. My black clogs lined up between the dusty boots of the man with white hair and the red-cherry spiked heels of the woman whose pageant-like appearance at nine in the morning scored way more points than my hospital scrubs and hair knotted in a bun. My face, neck, and ears felt impossibly hot, and I wasn't sure if it was because I wished I looked like her or because Ms. Webster, the teacher who years earlier had been with Gary Richard, was walking away from the podium.

I fantasized how to get even with her as she brushed a tight platinum blond curl out of her face and bent down to tell a squirmy little boy to keep his hands to himself. I smacked back in silence, *Why don't you!*

How could Gary Richard have been with her? How can she act as if everything is okay? I straightened my posture, wanting to call her bluff and announce to the parents, the students, the other teachers, "She isn't so righteous!"

Without warning, my mind spread images of Ian and various men across my table of conviction, and I stared at my knees. *Was my behavior any better?*

I pinned my arms against my stomach, seeing Daniel's fifth-grade teacher lean into the microphone. She announced Daniel's name and invited him to the stage. "Daniel has received all As for all four quarters this year."

Daniel leaped to his feet, lunged forward to shake her hand, then skipped up the stairs to take his place in the middle of the stage, pushing the paper out from his chest like he was Superman.

My spirit soared. *That's my boy!* I zoomed in on his face with the camera.

As I quietly marveled at the sight of him, I felt God dive in and speak to my heart. *Caroline, you will be okay. He, you, your family will do great things. I have you. I am with you.*

I inhaled deeply. The murmurs of students and teachers fell off in the distance as the silence of surrender expanded within my chest. I savored the presence I hadn't felt for over a year. I exhaled, whispering under my breath, "Thank you."

A short while later, back at work, I drummed my fingers against the desk as I waited for my next patient to enter my office. My mind wasn't on the patient, though. I was wondering how many of my friends and family had opened the email I just sent them. Would they wonder what happened when I told them how thankful I was for this day? Would they reply, wanting to know how I knew my kids and I would be okay or why I felt compelled to tell them that beauty and blessings exist in every day?

"Boodle," Regina said, leaning against the door frame in her green scrubs. Boodle was her nickname for me. It had no meaning, except she only gave nicknames to the people she loved. "He'll be in in a minute. He's waiting on his wife."

I nodded.

"I read your email." Her smile lit up her face. "We're thankful for you too."

I wiped a tear from my eye as surely as I had done when Regina delivered the barely used bed for Daniel or lent me $120 to pay the overdue water bill and another $40 to have them turn the water back on, knowing I couldn't repay her.

Her kindness never made sense to me, nor did Sue's or the other ladies I worked with who donated cash to wrinkle, twist, and shape into a money angel they gave me on Christmas. God's kindness didn't make sense to me either.

Why would He speak to me once, let alone twice? Had He not seen what I'd been doing? I wasn't the most faithful. The kids and I rarely went to church—most Sundays, we slept past ten. I didn't study His Word at four in the morning, as Regina did, or go to Mass, like Sue. I still prayed with the kids at night, though, so that was something, right?

I knew I hadn't entirely stopped believing in God after that Thanksgiving weekend in 2006, because that was who I'd cried out to in the shower. That was who I'd offered my tears to as I'd bitten my shirt to muffle the cries behind the bathroom door. Wondering. Pleading. Begging—for a life that didn't feel so heavy. Then in the next breath, I'd curse Him, because reality left the words of well-meaning folks—"God doesn't give you more than you can handle"—up for debate. But for whatever reason, He chose to return. And as I wasn't doing anything that could make Him go away, I needed Him to do something, to give me something in exchange for my good behavior. So I promised to forgive Ms. Webster because her sins weren't worse than my own. I vowed to give up dating, one-night stands, men, and sex until I entered another marriage and focus only on raising my kids. Swearing this time, I was ready to live God's way, even though I wasn't exactly sure what that meant. Or what I expected to receive for my good behavior.

Three months later, I enrolled in night classes to get a medical terminology certificate so I could apply for another job at the hospital that paid $2 more an hour. Three months after that, I got the job.

My last day working in my department, I stood inside the break room and stared at the sugary words woven into the white buttercream blanket covering my farewell cake. *Good luck, Caroline*, it read. *We will miss you.*

"Do you like it, Boodle?" Regina asked.

I smiled with a bittersweet feeling.

"I'm sad you're leaving me," she said. "But I am proud of you for doing what's best for you and the kids."

I responded with a slow nod. Words were stuck in my throat. How could I say goodbye to people who'd lived a lifetime alongside me? Memories of my coworkers flooded my mind: buying presents when Daniel turned five, crying with me when we thought Ember wasn't going to survive, gasping at Gary Richard's charges, placing pills in my hand to give my headache a rest, opening their ears, and closing doors when I needed the space to rage and let the anger out. They were a blessing in my life.

"You've got to promise to stop by and see us when you can. And you know Sue and I will still need you to help us old ladies understand that site where we have to enroll for our annual employee benefits. Dang technology."

I dug for a tissue and forced a chuckle. "I know."

"You still want me to keep the kids on New Year's Eve, right?"

"Of course. That's our tradition."

Over the next few months, as I settled into my new job, I felt my thoughts scatter. I was excited to make more money but felt somber that it still wasn't enough. I lit up each morning when my name greeted me on the wall of my cubicle, when I saw the beaming faces of the ladies I was starting to grow close to, and when my boss's eyes sparkled the same way my mom's did when the kids and I stopped by to visit. Yet at night, my face turned pallid when the sediment in the water heater sang a disturbing "boil-and-pop" lullaby and when the shadows moved slowly on the other side of the blinds. I'd jam my hands into my armpits, wishing I had someone to hold me when I didn't feel safe.

I knew God had a plan for us, and apparently my new boss did too. One day, she slid papers across my desk, saying, "I think you should apply. You'd be a great candidate for it, and I think it will help you and your kids in the future."

I glanced down at the papers. It was an application for a new program the hospital was starting called School at Work, to help guide staff who were interested in growing in their career or going back to school.

"But what about my work around here when I have class?"

"Don't worry about that. Just apply. If you get in, everyone will pitch in to help cover the hours you're away. The best part is you still get paid while you go to the classes."

I fidgeted with the pen, feeling humbled she believed in me more than I did. "Okay, I will fill it out and send it in."

I knew she was right, that it could help the kids and me, that even $12 an hour wasn't enough to support us or keep me from turning to payday loans to pick up the slack. But although I knew change was necessary, it didn't make it less scary to wait for the acceptance letter that came weeks after the kids and I celebrated one year inside our new home. It didn't make it less scary to dare to believe that I could learn new skills and grow in new ways without the guilt of leaving old things behind, like Gary Richard.

It had been more than a year since the kids had seen their dad. When we'd left the prison that November 2007, he wanted us to return *soon*, but in the busyness of a move, a job change, schooling, and parenting, *soon* turned into a year and five months later.

I knew the kids needed to see their dad—and he needed to see them. He darted across the room with eyes twinkling brighter than the last time we'd visited. He pulled out the chair between Ember and Daniel, whose face was solemn like the little boy I'd seen taking the photo when I came to pre-screen the prison. Gary Richard leaned toward Ember, whose splayed fingers covered her shy grin. "Do you like reading along with Daddy in those books I am sending?"

Rocking slightly in her chair, Ember smiled. "Yes, I like the princess one."

Sharing a happy glance as Ember looked at me, I knew how much she loved it; I had played the cassette tape again for the third time the previous night while she sat in my lap on the floor in her room, flipping the pages in the book as Gary Richard's recorded voice read to her.

"That's a neat reading program for them to offer the dads who are in here," I told Gary Richard. "It's a cool way for you to bond with the kids. They love getting the package in the mail."

He shook his head and muttered, "Yeah, but they don't have hardly any books for older kids." He turned toward Daniel. "I am trying to send you one, but they don't have anything to choose from that I think you would like. That last one I read seemed pretty childish for a smart boy like you."

Daniel shrugged half-heartedly.

"I've tried to call a few times. You guys are never home."

My voice felt flat. "Um, what do you expect? I work a lot. The kids usually eat dinner down at my parents'. A lot of nights, we aren't home until seven or eight."

"It makes it hard for me to talk to them."

I nodded, not feeling like having this conversation, or entertaining his unspoken demands.

"So why aren't you staying at a hotel this visit?" Gary Richard asked.

Without taking a breath, I ran my words together. "We have a lot going on right now between his weightlifting and baseball, her dance, their school, my work. I thought it would be best if we just headed back. Plus, right now, it's just something I can't afford."

"I wish I was there to help you, but there's not much I can do from inside here."

I lifted my palm up in a "who cares?" gesture, thinking my frustration would be less obvious to the kids that way than if I'd rolled my eyes.

Gary Richard stared up at the clock. "Next time, I hope you can stay longer."

The kids and I each took turns robotically hugging him goodbye. This visit was different from the last. Eyes stayed dry, conversations stalled, and they moved like they were bored. I wondered why.

As we made our way through the tunnel of barbed wire, something inside me shifted and replayed the way Daniel's arms hung limply at his sides after being wanded by the guard for drugs, the way he fidgeted with the quarters instead of looking for Gary Richard's face to appear in the window, and how the concrete was crunching under his feet. "Do you want to come back to visit your dad?"

His face flattened. "No."

On the drive home, we listened to music, stopped, and ate. Daniel shared fun facts about windmills as we each tried

to be the first to spot them, and I wondered if they remembered it was Gary Richard who taught us how to play this
game. We didn't talk about their dad, but we rarely did.
Between laughter and stories, I wondered what had changed
Daniel's mind. Maybe it was because he was almost a teen,
and prison was the last place he wanted to be. Maybe the
passage of time had turned his dad into a stranger. Perhaps he
never wanted to visit in the first place. Perhaps he was doing
okay, but I had never taken the time to ask because we were
always in a hurry.

Five hours later and back home, we said our prayers. I
turned out the lights in each of their rooms after kissing the
tops of their heads, then went to the bathroom to wash my
face.

I stared in the mirror and reflected on words from
another article I'd read recently. "Kids just need to know
they're safe. Safe to make mistakes. Safe to fly." Was seeing
their dad in prison safe? Did it promote growth and change?
Daniel's detached expression made it clear he didn't want to
go back. Although the statistics said that not seeing his dad
would leave a void I couldn't fill—that only his dad could—I
supported his decision.

I watched the shadows rise and fall outside and felt my
heart race, but who could I call? I was the one responsible for
the safety of us all. I closed my eyes. "Father, strengthen me to
be whatever superhero these children will more likely need."

CHAPTER 21

SUFFOCATE OR SURVIVE

You're sick! What kind of person sends a letter like this from prison? I dropped Gary Richard's letter onto the kitchen table and stared at it in disbelief. My eyes grew teary and hot as I reread his statement: *There isn't a man who sees a teenage girl and doesn't want to have sex with her.*

I looked away, despising how freely his disgusting words bled into the ones that described how much he missed the kids, the country love songs that reminded him of home, and how he couldn't wait to get out.

It's not okay to send a letter like this to me. It's not okay to think I would be okay with reading it. It's not okay that you believe all men think that about teenage girls. It's not okay—and the prison thinks you're ready to be released!

Weaving my hand into my hair, I pulled the roots tight. My mind rang with all the excuses I had made for his behavior over the years, believing that I was anchoring myself to some semblance of normalcy, safety, and a truth. All those times I'd compartmentalized the things I saw on the computer, his criminal behavior, and his charges, believing they didn't affect his ability to be a good father. All those times I'd believed that despite his destructive behaviors, somehow I'd still be able to co-parent responsibly beside this man, the man I had fixated on fourteen years before.

I grabbed the phone to call his parole officer, since Gary Richard was scheduled to be released soon, then paused as a cold realization washed over me: *If you do this, there is no turning back.* I closed my eyes, knowing I couldn't make an excuse this time. I was done.

As soon as Mr. Lawson answered the phone, I told him of my concerns. "Gary Richard sent me a letter. I thought the letters from the prison are screened, aren't they?"

"It is my understanding they do or at least try to."

"I think they must not have checked this one, because if they saw what he sent me, I am surprised they'd be okay with it—considering his charges and all."

"What did he send you?"

"Well." I swallowed. "H-he wrote something that really worries me." I looked at the first page of his five-page letter, then repeated what he'd written about all men wanting to have sex with teenage girls.

"Do you still have the letter?" His tone grew firm like my dad's when I was sixteen, telling me I was a little girl playing with fire.

"Yes."

"Can you bring it to my office?"

I chewed my inner cheek, knowing it wasn't a question.

"I will need the original. If you want, you can make copies before you bring it, or I can make copies for you when you drop it off. I will need the original and the envelope it came in, then I will call and discuss this with Mrs. Davis. Have you spoken with her?"

"No, is she still his parole officer? I thought you were his PO now."

"Since he's still on the inside, Mrs. Davis is his PO, and I take over once he is released. But I will contact her and let her know what is going on." I could hear the faint clicks of the keyboard. "You should know this will probably impact his release date."

I stared at the letter until the words began to blur. "Will he know I am the one who turned the letter in?"

"No! She will probably tell him the guards confiscated it during screenings; can't see her bringing your name into it, especially if it impacts his out date."

I breathed a sigh of relief and agreed to drop it off at his office in the morning. After hanging up, I leaned against the kitchen wall, feeling relieved yet unsure. I could tell by the urgency in Mr. Lawson's voice that Gary Richard's words were wrong. I knew I was doing the right thing, but I also remembered how it turned out the last time I'd walked into an office to *do the right thing.* That had led to the feeling Sergeant Long had betrayed my confidence.

The following day, I slid the handwritten, double-sided letter inside its envelope to the lady standing behind the window in the lobby of Mr. Lawson's office. *Am I doing the right thing?*

Her encouraging smile made me feel I was, but did that outweigh the risk? I wanted him to be held accountable for his words, but what would he do if he found out it was me? And worse, what was he going to do when I would no longer allow the kids to have contact with him? Although he would always be our children's father, I no longer believed having contact with him was in their best interest.

I didn't have the answers. The only thing I knew for certain was that his life and his dreams of seeing the kids when he got out were about to be ripped apart. I headed toward work, wondering how long it would take for them to confront Gary Richard and what I would say to him after they did.

Eight days passed without a word from Gary Richard, Mr. Lawson, or Mrs. Davis. The anxiety of wanting to know the result—and yet not wanting to know—was taking its toll. I struggled just to get out of bed every morning, showing up late to work several days in a row. Now here I was running late again. I raced out the door of my house, knowing I was going to be at least ten minutes late. I sped to the hospital and rushed inside to my department. The light outside my department's door seemed bright, as if those inside were waiting to interrogate me for my perpetual tardiness.

I pushed open the door, ready to offer a lie to anyone waiting on the other side. Instead of curious or accusing eyes, I saw nothing but a wide-open and empty path leading to my desk. Letting a sigh of relief escape my lips, I walked confidently toward my cubicle, feeling thankful and proud I hadn't gotten caught.

Just as I was taking my final steps, out of nowhere, my coworker Annie appeared, a frightened look in her eyes. "Gary Richard called here, Caroline!"

"What?" I stumbled back a few steps.

She nodded fiercely. "Just a few minutes ago!"

My eyes widened. "He knows?"

"What are you gonna say if he calls back?"

"I don't know." I looked away, feeling grateful that she knew my situation. Besides being a close coworker and friend, she knew a lot about the law, because her uncle was a high-rank-ing officer in our city.

For the next couple hours I did my best to focus on my job and not think about Gary Richard's call—or that he would certainly try it again. But when my cell phone began to vibrate in my purse at 10:18 a.m., I knew instinctively the time of our showdown had arrived. I grabbed my purse and plunged my fingers in to retrieve the phone. Then I pulled my headset off and dropped it onto my desk.

"Annie!" I whispered loudly.

She tilted the microphone attached to her headset away from her mouth. "What?"

"I think this is him." I lifted my phone so she could see the screen displaying the words *Private Number*.

Her eyes grew overly bright, like the blue flame on a stove. "Go. Go. I'll cover for you."

Racing into the conference room across the hall, I slipped between rows of empty tables and stacks of chairs and tucked myself in a nook along the wall. "Hello."

"Ms. Downey? This is Mr. Lawson."

I breathed a sigh of relief that it wasn't Gary Richard.

"Ms. Downey, I am calling because I want you to hear this from me. I assured you that Gary Richard wouldn't know you were the one who turned in the letter. However, I just found out from Mrs. Davis that Ms. Wood, who is in charge of the rehabilitation program he attends, told him it was you."

I pulled my legs closer together in shock at yet another betrayal I'd suffered at the hands of the authorities.

"I'm not sure what happened, other than there was a miscommunication between Mrs. Davis and Ms. Wood. Ms. Wood is the one who met with him to discuss the letter, and somewhere in the conversation, she mentioned that his ex-wife reported it."

"So she just threw me under the bus?"

"Ms. Downey, I am sorry. I don't know why this happened, but I wanted to let you know."

My jaw tensed as my mind exploded into a raging fire. *Sorry? You're sorry! This isn't a game—this is my life. Why would she do that? I should have known this would happen.* "Well, *you* should know that he called my work this morning. They didn't accept the call."

"If he calls back, you don't have to talk with him," Mr. Lawson advised.

A short burst of nervous laughter escaped my lips. "Yeah, I do."

"I am deeply sorry, Ms. Downey."

Easy for you to say. You'll get off this call and go about your life. I'm the one who has to pick up the pieces of the mess you all caused.

"Feel free to call if you need anything."

My eyes nearly rolled into the back of my head. I had already done that—and look what it had gotten me!

I hung up and tossed the phone beside me, then I crossed my arms around my knees in a protective huddle. *What am I going to do?*

Letting anger guide me, I grabbed my phone, searched for Mrs. Davis's number, and called. It went straight to voicemail. "Mrs. Davis, this is Caroline Downey. I need to speak with you regarding Gary Richard. I heard from Mr. Lawson that you, well, Ms. Wood told him it was me. I need to talk to someone. Please call me back."

Next I began flicking through websites of attorneys to sue the state for putting me in harm's way. After looking through a few, I glanced at the time. I'd been away from my desk for thirty minutes.

I need to get back.

As I hurried down the hall, my phone rang again. *Must be Mrs. Davis.* I answered quickly, not giving the ID number much thought.

"This is a call from . . . Gary Richard . . . an inmate at a correctional institution," the robotic voice announced. I pressed the button to accept and then sprinted outside, bracing myself for what I knew was coming.

"I can't believe you turned in my letter! You're a b—"

I held the phone in the air, trying to shield myself from the profanity he was spitting out. And although my heart was racing, I wasn't scared. I didn't cringe as he called me names. I didn't cower as I had behind our couch almost four years before, watching spit build in the corners of his mouth. Instead, I rolled my eyes and shook my head, admiring how the sunlight speckled my shirt like glitter.

"They pulled my date. But I bet you're happy about that, aren't you?"

I gave a curt nod but didn't speak.

"I'm sure that's what you wanted—to keep me in here, isn't it?" Then, as though arrogantly egging me on, he drew out his words. "Huh? Huh? Answer me! Isn't it?" His voice took on a tart tone, and I knew he was sneering, just as he had the night he slid the box cutter blade across his wrist. "Yeah, this is exactly what you wanted."

I'd had enough. "What I wanted?" I snapped back at him. "None of this is what *I* wanted."

I didn't want the circles under my eyes that continued to darken every night as I stayed up doing homework, desperately trying to complete the final year of an associate degree or study-ing to sit for my coding certification. I didn't want four hours of sleep, multiple jobs, every minute accounted for, because I was trying to parent and do everything on my own. I didn't want to bark orders at the kids before we walked in the door or have the guilt of not being home more for them. I didn't want to sink in shame the previous Friday at the salon when the lady with tinfoil hair sitting beside me cracked jokes about the stu-pidity of people who live off payday loans, knowing Monday morning I'd have to get another one. I didn't want my strength consumed fighting to break cycles so the kids could have a bet-ter life, and although I loved them deeply, I had never wanted to parent them alone.

Gary Richard's shouts grew louder, and even though I kept the phone at a distance, I could still hear his booming voice piercing through the busy parking lot. "You know, it's funny. Everyone thinks you're so sweet. So innocent. You tell everyone I'm a liar, but you're the one who said you would never keep the kids away from me."

I glanced around, hoping nobody could hear, then I offered a smile that held heartbreak, amusement, and bitterness all at once. "What you said in that letter isn't right. Do you realize our son is thirteen? And has teenage friends? And that even though Ember is only six, she will one day too. So until you can become a stable, responsible, contributing member of society, I am not allowing you to have any more contact with them."

"Caroline, you know that is not what I meant."

"No, I don't."

"What I wrote isn't what I meant, and I can't believe you are using that to keep my kids from me. You said you would never do that because they need a father."

I squeezed my eyes shut. "They do need a father—or a father figure—but until you can show that you have changed, that you have something positive to add to their lives, I am not allowing it."

"So you're just going to ruin my life like that."

"I am not trying to ruin your life. You are their dad, and they love you. At night we still pray for you, and I still don't talk bad about you around them, but I am no longer living like this."

I felt immune to muffled pleas. For the first time, confronting him, I held my posture straight and my head high. "I wish you the best, Gary Richard, but I can't keep doing this. I won't put them through this."

"I would never do anything to hurt my kids." His voice cracked.

"Your *actions* hurt us!" I took a deep breath to calm myself, then spoke slowly to emphasize my words. "So like I said, until you can show you have become a stable, responsible, contributing member of society, there will be no contact."

He let out a theatrical groan. "I have rights, and you can't keep them from me. At least not when I get out. I will get a lawyer."

"You can do whatever you need to do. I am not going to listen to your threats. I am going back to work."

I hung up and headed back inside. *Why can't he accept it? Why do his choices, his words, his actions rob me of mine?* I didn't want to explain to the kids why there wouldn't be another letter addressed to them waiting on the counter. Why, after a long night of baseball games, they wouldn't hear him enthusiastically say his name on the answering machine. I didn't want to explain why he didn't get out, why he could never come to their school or do all the things promised. One day, would the kids feel that my actions hurt them too?

Before I went inside, I needed to make a few of my own calls to attorneys. But after talking to two different ones and a retired paralegal, I was certain that I didn't have a winnable case. I walked with a slow, heavy step toward the entrance.

My phone rang again. I knew from the number it was a payday lender calling because my payment was late. I couldn't answer. I needed more time—another lie to hide the truth of my actions. *You can't keep doing this. You can't keep taking out loans to get by. You swore after the bankruptcy you wouldn't live like this again.*

Before I knew it, I was sitting slumped in my chair with my head propped on my hand, waiting for Annie to finish her call so I could tell her what had happened—but only about what had happened with Gary Richard. It was easier to discuss his actions. If I confessed to everything, she would know the truth, and that felt worse than his lies. My entire office would finally realize I was stupidly paying 300 percent interest over and over—they would talk about me the way the lady at the salon had talked about those "stupid people." They would pucker their faces in pity and judgment. They would know I wasn't doing as fine as I pretended to be. And they would know I was an impostor, because as much as I boasted that "God has a plan," I still struggled to believe in it.

Annie kept glancing over with eyes that said, *Almost done.* I just gave a half grin, admiring how the diamonds on her wedding ring sparkled under the glare of her screen while her fingers danced on top of the keys. I began fidgeting with my finger, fantasizing about wearing her ring and what it must have been like ten years ago when she married the man of her dreams. *Why couldn't I have had a life like hers?* I inhaled deeply and trapped all the air inside, as I realized I had a choice: I could suffocate under the dreams of the life I didn't get, or survive in the one I did.

CHAPTER 22

WHO I AM

"Do you know who I am?" asked the ghost-faced kid standing stiff at my parents' front door on Halloween 2015, waiting for my mom to guess while she dropped a handful of mini-sized candy bars in his bag.

"Umm . . . a scary ghost?" my mom said, pressing her palm against her chest, knowing it was one of my cousin's kids but still playing along.

My sister and I, sitting at the dining room table, paused our conversation to watch as Charlie raised his mask.

"Charlie, you tricked me!" Mom said with a smile.

I gave a half grin at the way he skipped off the porch so happy he'd fooled her, believing his mask made him unrecognizable. As Mom walked back into the bathroom to finish getting ready, I started to think about Darryl—a man I'd recently been dating and had broken up with. I had met him three months prior, through a mutual friend, and we had been inseparable since then; I felt unrecognizable now that we were no longer in a relationship.

"I don't understand," I said to Blair, resting my chin in the palm of my hand. "It's like I gravitate to the guys who have issues, and I reject the decent ones. Like Sam." Sam worked with Annie's husband. "Why couldn't I just like Sam?"

Blair grinned. "Because you said he was too nice and he wore his hat too much."

"I know! What does that even mean? He's such a nice guy. He's an amazing dad, loves his parents, is involved at his church—and I ruled him out after four weeks. But with Darryl, I overlooked everything." I rolled my eyes.

She shrugged, and I silently replayed how Darryl would watch television with a beer propped between his legs, too distracted to interact with his kids or with me. How he never had anything positive to say about people or life. How I pretended with a smile to be okay with his drinking, his anger, his driving me around when I knew he had too much to drink. And yet I gave him everything, including sex.

"I still can't believe I introduced him to my kids." I shook my head. "But I just knew he was *the one* after that first date when he took me hiking through the woods, because he planned something different from just going to dinner." I made a *tsk*ing sound. "A hat, a freaking hat—and I reject Sam. What is wrong with me?"

"I don't think anything is wrong with you. Maybe you're just not ready to date?" Blair said.

"Maybe, but how much longer do I need to wait? It's been eight years since my divorce." I chuckled. "Maybe I don't know how."

"Well, don't ask me. I've been married eighteen years," she said with a wide grin.

The doorbell rang.

Mom came waltzing out of the bathroom wearing cutoff denim overalls over a bright multicolor jumpsuit, with her face painted like a clown. Without missing a beat, she twirled around and scooped up the bowl of candy.

"Trick or treat!" The high-pitched voices of children rang out, making me think about how, in years past, I couldn't wait to see what Mom and Dad would be dressed as when they came to the parties Gary Richard and I hosted each Saturday before Halloween. Or what Blair said about being married eighteen years. That was how long Gary Richard and I would have been married, if we had lasted.

Eighteen years. So much had visibly changed since that summer in 1997 when we married. Daniel was eighteen with bulky athletic shoulders, a full beard, and thighs the size of tree trunks. He'd graduated from high school in May and moved into the college dorms in August, where he was playing football and studying biology. Ember was twelve, with yellow-brown hair that fell delicately past her petite waist and a shy smile that belied her adventurous spirit. I turned thirty-six in September. And Gary Richard? I couldn't really say. After that summer in 2010 when he sent the letter, I refused any more contact with him.

Over the months and years since then, he'd occasionally attempted to reach out through phone calls, so I'd blocked the number. Or I'd get an update from the automated victim services hotline I registered with, letting me know of his release from prison in February 2011. Then a short time later, he violated his parole for failing to register as a sex offender and ended up back in prison for another two years. Every so often, I'd hear from acquaintances or read online sources that indicated he was in more trouble, with new charges filed. Or child support enforcement would notify me regarding his repeated violations for nonsupport of the kids. Each time I'd roll my eyes at his one-foot-always-inside-the-prison behavior, convinced that time would never break that pattern, because he was unwilling or didn't know how to change. But with each new snippet of news, I knew I'd made the right decision to remove him from our lives.

Blair returned to the table, pulling me back into the present. "You look deep in thought."

"Yeah, something like that." I paused, feeling a cringe of regret for the time I couldn't get back. "You know before I started talking to Sam, it had been six years since I dated, or had time to talk to someone, like really trying to get to know them." I sighed. "I really thought I was ready—especially now that my life looks like I wanted it to, with my career and all. I love what I do. And with the money I'm making, I can pay my bills before the due date." I let out a slight chuckle. "I paid last month's electric bill nearly a week early." I raised my palm as if I were swearing in a testimony. "I have never done that!"

She smiled. "That's good."

"I still can't believe my credit score was finally good enough for me to get a new car." Then, as quickly as the words exited, my pulse started to pick up as an unwelcome ache entered. "I guess I thought . . . it would all feel different now."

I turned in my seat, losing the thread of the conversation as I spotted Dad lost in the land of the television, and I felt envious of the way he could block everything out and just *be*. I wished I could do that—sit without thoughts that raced to the next and the next, as though fighting to get to a finish line that kept moving. Always convincing myself that if I did this, that would happen, and when I got over there, if I just got over there, then life would finally be what I wanted it to be—this self-produced guarantee woven into every promise I made to God, my children, and myself.

Like when I promised after Gary Richard was out of our lives, I wouldn't crawl back to the behaviors that kept me stuck, only to find myself living again off payday lenders instead of within my means and heading right back to the same lawyer to file another bankruptcy in 2014.

Or when I promised my kids I'd have more time to spend with them after I finished my degree and began working from home, only to be seduced by overtime and the opportunity to afford things we never could. But now I didn't have that luxury because Daniel was away at college.

Or when I promised God that I'd forgive Gary Richard, Sergeant Long, and the others who wronged me so I could get a life of ease for my righteous behavior, only to feel defeated when I didn't.

Blair cleared her throat, pulling me back into the conversation. "Different how? Like that you would have met someone by now?"

"Yes, a little of that." I fidgeted with my empty ring finger.

She fixed her gaze on my hand. "Maybe next time just trust your gut about them in the beginning. Do you realize that since you started dating again, you always call me early on after meeting them, to tell me about things you're questioning, but then talk yourself out of it? Like when you called to ask if someone drinking a twelve-pack of beer a day might indicate a drinking problem."

I let out a short burst of embarrassed laughter, then shrugged. "It all just feels so confusing. I know how to be when it's just the kids and me, but when I start to date, it's like I don't know who I am. It's like I get lost. Did I ever tell you what Brad said to me one time?"

Her eyebrows squished together in thought. "Wait! Which one was Brad?"

"The guy from Minnesota. You know, the one I met at that charity basketball game who was here visiting his brother?"

"Kind of."

"We didn't date that long. But one night he started teasing me about how quickly I leaned in to kiss him when I picked him up just days after he approached me at that game. When I did it, he pushed me back, saying, 'Whoa.' I felt embarrassed because, from our conversations, I assumed he wanted the kind of girl who would go after what she wants. But as he was teasing me, his voice got serious, and he asked if I had ever done any self-help type of work or gone to counseling."

Blair raised her eyebrows. "What did you say?"

"I didn't say anything. I was so mad I couldn't. He had no clue about all the things I've been through or the countless hours I have spent watching self-help videos and reading books trying to fix myself and grow. But I listened to him anyway. He told me he knew I didn't give my own opinions when he asked me questions. But the part that hurt, that really stuck in my head, was when he said he thought I was the kind of girl who would go along with and do whatever a man said just to please them instead of being who I am."

I looked down, then back up at Blair, whose lips pressed tightly together as if she was mad or trying to understand. Then, with a thin voice, I said, "Maybe he is right. Because when I was with Darryl, or even Sam, it was like I didn't know who I was supposed to be. I still feel that way." Water began to fill my eyes. "I know how to take care of my kids. I know how to work. I know how to be the *me* who does all those things, but maybe I don't know how to be *just me*."

She reached over and rubbed my back while Mom quietly slid next to me at the table and clutched my hand with her red fingernails.

"I do feel blessed with everything I have, I really do, but it still feels like something is missing. Like . . ." I searched for words. "Like there's something wrong with me."

I closed my eyes and rubbed my forehead as I thought of Brad, Darryl, Sam, Ian, the men before him, including Gary Richard, and the boys before him. Had I always been reaching for a man's acceptance? A slow smile crept across my face as I made a realization. "I feel like I need to go to church."

Blair quickly leaned over, reaching for her phone. "Did you get the text on our friends group chat that Heather sent, wanting to know if any of us want to go to church with her?"

"I don't think so. When did she send it?"

"Earlier today." Blair ran her finger over the screen of her phone. "Here. See?"

I read the text and grinned, knowing this message wasn't a coincidence. God had used the timing and our conversation to get me to recognize something I'd been missing for far too long.

I grabbed my phone from my purse to see if Heather had sent me a message. She hadn't, which confirmed God's timing even more. I texted Heather that I would like to join her one Sunday.

Heather replied later that evening, saying she planned to go Sunday, November 8, to a church her friend from our high school had planted and was pastoring. That Sunday morning, I decided to check out the church without Ember, much like I did the prison. Not sure why exactly. I wasn't worried that the environment would be too scary for a child, but with a preteen, I did worry she'd give me grief about having to wake up early on a Sunday to hear a monotone pastor talk in words that went over her head—which was what I had done to my parents when I was growing up. Perhaps, though, it was simply because we hadn't been to a church consistently since we'd prayed with Pastor Bob in our church lobby the winter of 2006. Now nine years later, I didn't know what to expect.

Breathe, Caroline. Just breathe, I told myself as I got out of my car and headed toward the church entrance.

"Hey, girl! How are you?" Heather said with a smile, meeting me a few cars down. She leaned in to hug me.

"I am doing good."

"You remember Mike from high school?"

"Yeah. We weren't close or anything but ran in the same circles of people. I was surprised to hear he is a pastor now."

"Yeah," she said, flashing a crooked grin. "We all were. He and I have been close friends for years, and believe me, out of all our friends from high school, he is the last one I thought would be a pastor." She laughed. "It's neat, though, seeing him all grown up like this and seeing how much God has changed his life. I have heard him officiate some weddings and a funeral. He does such a good job speaking. You're going to love him. I have been saying forever that I wanted to check out his church, but I haven't ever had anyone to go with me— and it felt weird for me to come alone—so I'm glad we get to do this together."

The aroma of brewed coffee greeted us as we entered the lobby. I didn't expect that. Nor did I anticipate how cool the building's design would be. "Wow," I said, noticing the wooden chairs arranged in rows facing the stage. "These chairs are so trendy. In my old church, we just had pews." The stage had a neon backdrop that glowed behind a band whose style looked as hip as the room.

"Ember will love this! She likes those kinds of lights." I pointed at the filament inside the clear bulbs dangling throughout the sanctuary.

We made our way past welcoming faces of every age. Everyone seemed friendly and happy.

We took seats about halfway back and settled in for the service. I sat in stunned silence, taking it all in—nothing about the building or what it contained matched any of the churches I had been to before. Where were the pews, the organ, the stained-glass windows, the cross on the steeple, or . . . the steeple? Where were the tattered hymnals, the choir dressed in robes, the wooden pulpit, or the baptismal pool? I could feel my chest expand in the wonder of it all as my eyes grew bright thinking how much Ember, who had a passion for interior design, would enjoy seeing the creativity inside this space.

Feeling a firm touch on my right shoulder, I turned and found myself staring into emerald eyes. They cut right through me.

"Hi, I'm Zach. I'd like to give you a card to fill out so we can get to know you," he said, placing a card in my hand.

My breath hitched at his attractiveness, the confidence in his voice, the way it seemed he was delivered straight from heaven. I swallowed, wanting to say, "Do I bring this back to you?" but all I could do was smile.

As he walked away, I shifted in my chair, staring past the program Heather held in her hand. My thoughts staggered between wondering what was in the program and wondering what it was about this place that made me feel so at home.

Was it Zach's lingering smile, the coffee, or something else? Just then, the background music began to fade, then seamlessly grew louder as a woman with straight hair strummed the guitar. Pastor Mike, wearing skinny jeans and a button-up shirt, walked forward and stood at the front row.

We rose as if we were in the standing-only section of a concert, and with the power of the band's vocals pounding through the sound system, I felt like I was. Barely moving my lips, I sang along with the words on the projection screen. It seemed as though each lyric was written for me. With a wandering gaze, I watched hands rise around the room, then caught Zach staring at me, causing a jittery feeling to trickle down my spine. I quickly turned my attention back to the front, where Pastor Mike's arms were flying high over his head like a kite dancing in the wind. I couldn't see his eyes, but instinctively I felt they were closed, and I wondered where he went. What place had he gone in his mind that made him free enough to raise his arms in praise like that and not worry about someone's judgment? I wondered if he felt that same peace I had felt before at the awards assembly at Daniel's school. If so, could he help me get it back?

When he got up to speak, I wasn't sure what to expect exactly, but I was amazed by his teaching style. He explained the Bible in a way that made it easy to understand. And he related it to our times. I felt as though he was talking right to me. I loved it. And I knew Ember would too.

After the service, Heather and I made our way toward Pastor Mike and waited our turn, along with several others, to talk to him.

"Hey, it's good to see you both," Mike said, his eyes lighting up in recognition, when we finally got in front of him.

"Your sermon was good," Heather said, and I gave a crisp nod.

"I haven't seen you in a long time." He directed his questioning eyes at me.

"I know," I said casually. "Probably since high school. This is a really cool place you have here. I was telling Heather my daughter will love it. She is almost a teenager."

He smiled warmly. "Thanks! I'm glad you liked it. I hope to see you again, maybe next Sunday?"

"Yes, and I will bring her with me."

As Heather and I made our way toward the exit, I slowed down my stride, almost catlike, as I glanced around the room for Zach. When I spotted him toward the back of the room bundling ink pens, I pivoted away from Heather. "Hang on," I told her.

I held out the card. "Um. Hi, I got this all filled out."

"Oh, okay," he said, placing those sharp eyes on me. "Thank you! Hope you ladies have a great day."

Heather and I walked outside, and now clearly out of anybody's earshot, I exclaimed, "Well, he is cute!"

We both laughed before parting ways, agreeing to see each other the next Sunday, which we did—and many Sundays after that, as Ember and I dived in, rarely missing a service. I volunteered to serve in the mornings, hoping to learn more about the church and the people there, like Zach and if he was single. With each week that passed, I yearned to know more about him, eagerly returning just to be near him. I also wanted to know more about this God Pastor Mike spoke of, the One who seemed more relational than transactional. His sermons had a way of bringing the Bible to life, making it relatable to the restlessness, temptations, doubts, and fears I faced each day.

One evening, a few months later, while Ember was with friends, I sprawled across the love seat, feeling alone, listening to music stream from my phone. I just felt blah as I shuffled aimlessly through songs. My thoughts accused me of all the reasons I still wasn't enough.

A delicate singing voice broke through my thoughts.

I sat up straight, narrowing my eyes on the phone screen to read the song title: "Need You Now" by Plumb. I listened intently to every syllable.

Tears started cascading down as I cried out to God, "Who are You? And who am I? Why am I so messed up?" I closed my eyes in the unknowingness of it all.

Over the years, I thought I had surrendered my life to God before, but I still struggled. I thought if I believed in God, I would always feel whole. On any given Sunday, I felt holy, but by Sunday night, I craved the touch of a man. Come Monday, I was grateful for what my life looked like; by Monday night, I wished my life looked more like my sister's life. Tuesday, I wanted to be serious, then by Wednesday, I only had the capacity for corny. Thursday morning, I felt strong, then by Friday night, I was scared as I lay in bed watching the mysterious shadows rise and fall. A walking contradiction. Could I be all these things?

The following day, I felt an unshakable urge to message Pastor Mike. *I would like to meet with you.* I typed the words, then reread them, deleted them, and then closed my eyes, taking in a long, slow breath. I started again: *I would like to meet with you sometime to share my story.*

Pastor Mike messaged back within the hour, and we scheduled a time for me to come to his house to speak with him and his wife. A few days later, I arrived at their home, feeling thankful he was willing to allow me to come. My heart raced, realizing I had no idea what I was here to say or do, so I leaned my forehead against the steering wheel and prayed, "Lord, I am here because I believe this is where You want me to be. Let the words You want me to say come out."

Pastor Mike greeted me at the door, and I followed him to the sitting room, where his lovely wife, Ava, offered me something to drink. Sitting on a couch that lined up against the front windows, I listened as Pastor Mike rocked slightly in the recliner and told Ava, who sat in the chair next to him, how we used to go to high school together. For a few minutes, he and I reminisced about the *old days*.

"Did you know I used to hang out at Gary Richard's apartment back in the day?"

I tilted my head in surprise. "You did? I never knew that."

"Yeah. One time he pulled out a magazine that had a guy with no shirt and, like, ripped abs. He said it was him, that he was the model, but I was never quite sure if he was telling the truth or not."

I smirked. "You and me both."

"Oh, you saw it too?"

I let out a short, gloomy laugh. "Kind of what attracted me to him." Then without warning, tears began to build. I turned my head and brushed my cheeks, wishing I hadn't pulled all my hair back in a ponytail so I could use it to hide my face.

Ava slid tissues into my hand.

"Do you want to talk about it?" Pastor Mike asked kindly.

I nodded, knowing I had to get all this heaviness out of me. I swallowed, then I told them how Gary Richard and I met and why we got married. I explained about his charges, jail, and the letter. Wiping my tears, I glanced at them, expect-ing to see signs of shock, judgment, or disgust. All I saw was acceptance. So I clutched the tissue tighter, and I continued. I told them about my egg donations, struggles with money and promiscuity, the guilt I still carried, and how I felt that I was to blame for it all. They just sat, listening even when I was quiet, and I was thankful they didn't try to fill the silence with Scriptures or advice.

When I finished sharing, Pastor Mike said he knew some families who felt blessed by egg donors and what a gift that was to the many who struggled to have babies. I was one of those people who made it possible for them.

His words were what I needed to hear.

Ava smiled sweetly and looked me in the eyes. "You said you feel guilt, but do you feel shame about the donations?"

I felt heat flush through my body, as if everything inside was running around trying to hide. "No," I said sharply. Then without breaking eye contact, I continued, "I have regrets and guilt, but no, not shame."

We talked a bit more, and I felt grateful again that they didn't try to "fix" or overpower me with super spiritual talk. They gave me space to share, and they truly listened. Ava invited me to the women's group she was hosting in a few days, and I agreed to join her. It was such a gift.

As I left their home, I felt lighter, proud of myself for being brave enough to share my story and not second-guess-ing what I had exposed. But her question stuck with me, and I wondered what it meant for me.

A few days later, I walked up the sidewalk holding an over-thought store-bought snack for the women's group, debating with myself if it was too late to back out. I didn't know these ladies, but I knew I needed to do uncomfortable things to try and grow past the box my fears had placed me in.

The warmth of these ladies' smiles made me feel welcomed. I placed the food on the kitchen counter and made my way to a wooden chair that sat at the side of the living room. I watched as the women gathered, chatting and eating. While engaging in short "How are you?" conversations, I overheard one lady tell another that she saw Zach at the store with a woman.

Of course he is married. Strange she doesn't come with him to church. If I were his wife, he would never have to go alone.

Minutes later, the ladies in the kitchen and down the hall began nestling next to each other on the sofa, while others stretched their legs across the floor, and somehow I started to feel a little more comfortable in the room filled with strangers.

After showing the DVD Bible study, they handed out a card with different questions to each of us. My question asked if I felt discontentment, and if so, how did that tie into a desire for God's purpose? Such personal questions. How would I answer something so personal in a public way?

We got started with the discussion—a much deeper conversation than "How are you?"—as one by one the women answered their questions. I listened to each woman respond to ways they longed to see more of God in their lives, or how they worried how they'd sound if they spoke their dreams out loud, or that they questioned if they had missed God's purpose for them. I realized that they too had fears like my own. One lady's voice crackled as she admitted she felt unqualified to answer her question because it was tough.

These women are just like me.

Before coming here, I didn't expect any similarities between us, because each Sunday when I saw them, I wrote a narrative about them based on what I believed.

I'd cast the lady who sat on the right of the couch, centrally positioned in front of the large windows, as the "perfect one." She had it all together, and her life was free from struggle. She had money, a career, a successful marriage. Draped in fine jewelry, high-end clothes, and perfect hair. But when she spoke of heartbreak, loss, and confusion, I could see she was, in fact, the same as me.

The lady sitting diagonally from me was the character full of faith. She volunteered her time to serve in the church, referenced God with her words, backed up her belief with her actions. Scripture flowed beautifully from her lips, and her connection with God seemed more rooted than I would ever have. But when she spoke of doubts and fears, I could see she too was no different from me.

Woman after woman, each of whom I believed had reached a level of flawlessness in which they were spiritually exempt from temptation and sin, still battled with conflicting thoughts within. They worried about the same things I did—from finances to parenting to careers to finding balance in their daily schedules. The more they shared and the more I realized our similarities, the more I began to wonder, How do I get beautifully wise words to flow out as they do?

When it was my turn to share, I thought I should tell them about this unsettling feeling that I believed God was telling me to share my story with others. But when I felt their stares turn to me, I felt like that young girl again, standing in the doctor's office, believing he read my chart labeled Young, Dumb, and Pregnant.

My face grew hot as I tried to quiet my inner thoughts: *You're going to sound stupid. You're not as good as they are. Nobody cares what you have to say.* Finally, I mumbled, "Umm. Oh gosh, that's a tough one. I don't really know." I shrugged, then smiled, hoping that would mask my pain. "I am gonna have to think about it. That video was good, though."

The conversation moved on, and as I sat with a tight-lipped smile waiting to hear how the rest of the women would answer, I drifted back to what Brad said about not being who I was, then to Ava's question about shame. Were they both right?

After the evening ended, the questions lingered. Was shame the thing that made me think their responses, their opinions, mattered more than mine? Was it why I couldn't see the same beauty within me as I saw within them?

Later that night, after tucking Ember in and saying our prayers, I searched the internet for information on shame. I came across a TED Talk by Brené Brown in which she explained that guilt was "I did something bad," while shame was "I am bad."

My eyes focused intently on the screen as a haunting feeling closed in on me. Out of nowhere, I heard the words Sergeant Long spoke to me that day when I gave my statement about Gary Richard: *The only difference between you and the other girls is that he married you.*

I gave a slow nod, acknowledging the truth for the first time. I had been sixteen at the time. And just because I had wanted Gary Richard didn't mean he shouldn't have stopped it. I wasn't wrong or the one to blame. Nor did my past mean I had to spend my life shackled to shame, believing I was flawed. I was a victim, but I was also a victor. I was a little girl searching for love, but I was also the lover. And I was a mother and an independent woman. I smiled at the ceiling, feeling a shift in my perspective. I didn't have to hide parts of me to be accepted or seen, because *who I am* is *all* of those things. *And all of those things make me the strong woman I am today.*

CHAPTER 23

THE EVIDENCE
OF BLESSINGS

"Heather! Guess who just called me and asked me to go for coffee?" I asked.

"Who?"

"Zach!" I was on my way to pick up Ember from a friend's house one Sunday afternoon in mid-January 2017.

"I thought he was dating someone or married?"

"No, he was in a long-term relationship, but he isn't anymore. I'm telling you, Heather, there is something about him." I let out a whimsical sigh. "I really believe he's the one. I mean, what better place to meet your husband than at church?"

"True, but just take it slow. It's only coffee."

I giggled. *This is so much more than* only *coffee.*

For the last year I had chased his every glance, clung to his every word, fallen in love as I wrote about him in my journal, and prayed that God would bring us together. This wasn't *only* anything. This was confirmation.

"I know," I told her. "But for the last year, I have been praying for God to send me a husband, and something has drawn me to Zach since the day I walked in the doors of the church. If I'm honest, he is one of the reasons I kept coming back to church, at least in the beginning."

Heather chuckled. "Glad he kept you coming back."

"I'm so glad you invited me that first Sunday. It has definitely changed my life for the better." I glanced heavenward, feeling such gratitude, then settled my eyes back to the road. "I am glad he finally asked me out, because these past few months have been driving me crazy. The way he stares at me makes me feel like he is interested in me. But some days it's hard to tell. This morning, though, after the way he touched my back when he scooted next to me to ask if I could help him bundle papers . . ." I paused, remembering the way the tingles felt as they tickled my neck. "It was like I knew this was going to happen."

"I'm happy that now you don't have to drive yourself crazy wondering. Nobody deserves to find a man who's crazy in love with you more than you."

The following evening Zach greeted me at the coffee shop with those same intoxicating emerald eyes. For the next several hours, until the coffee shop closed, our conversation flowed seamlessly from topic to topic. We talked about our belief in God, then we shared about our past relationships. He complimented me about how good my children were, mentioning that he didn't have any of his own. It brought comfort that he didn't seem to mind that I had kids. After sharing an embrace in the parking lot, we agreed to meet the next afternoon for a walk.

The following week we shared dinners, more walks, and late-night talks on the phone that lasted until the wee hours of the morning. I felt like a giddy teenager with him, and when I was alone, I fell more in love as I journaled how an hour, forty-three minutes, and fifty-three seconds on the phone wasn't nearly long enough.

One night about two weeks after our coffee date, he greeted me at my door with flowers. "Now I know where my rib went," he told me, referencing a story from the Bible about how God took a rib from Adam to create Eve. I was hooked.

I was grateful we had known each other as friends for a year before we began dating. It made me feel more comfortable around him. And for the first time, I felt as though I could really be myself. We shared time at family weddings and birthdays; he watched Ember dance and Daniel play football. Everything about us felt so natural, so right, so perfect—as though my fairy-tale ending was finally coming true. So I was surprised when, on the Saturday after Easter, about three months into our relationship, he asked to stop by to talk.

I agreed, since Ember was at a friend's house, but swallowed hard, hearing distance in his voice.

"What's wrong?" I asked, when he showed up a half hour later.

Zach folded his hands in his lap and looked distraught and uneasy. "I can't do this anymore."

"Do what?"

"This. Us. I can't explain it. It isn't anything to do with you; it's me. This doesn't work for me."

Wrapping my arms around my body to insulate myself, I tried to make sense of what he was saying between long pauses and broken sentences. Then he started reciting Scriptures about lust.

With a tart tone, I cut him off. "Are you saying this thing between us is only about lust to you? Not love?"

He raised his head, eyes filled with pain. "Yes."

I sat in stunned silence, feeling broken, bruised, used.

He finally stood, as if to go.

"So that's it? You don't have anything else to say? You're just going to leave?"

He nodded slowly and walked out the door.

I slammed it behind him, then slid down the wall, burying my face in my hands, feeling like that same stupid, powerless teen with the chart labeled Dumb. "You said you loved me," I said through sobs. "You told me I was the one."

How did I get here again? The woman, the toy, the fool, the clown caught in another circus of lies. I thought I was worthy of something different this time.

After I cried until I had nothing left, I pulled off the wall the canvas artwork he had given me and sliced holes in it. I packed in a box his speaker and the jewelry and clothes he gave me, trying to rid the house of any trace of him.

By the time Ember came home, it was as if Zach never existed.

The following morning, as Ember and I made our way to church, I wondered if he would show up, but the service came and went with no sign of him. I wanted to ask Pastor Mike if he knew anything, but I didn't want to explain what happened because I wasn't sure what *had* happened.

Another Sunday came and went, with still no sign of Zach and no mention of him, except for one lady in our small group who told me that sometimes men just needed space and to be patient.

Maybe she was right, so I prayed that God would help him see that I was the right woman for him, that together he and I could do big things for the Lord.

Yet another Sunday with no Zach came. I sent him a text telling him I hoped he was doing okay and that I trusted I was not the reason he wasn't coming to church.

He responded a few days later, saying he was doing okay, and thanked me for reaching out. We agreed to meet so I could return his gifts and the things he had left. And secretly I hoped that seeing me one more time might change his mind.

Breathe, Caroline, just breathe, I recited as I topped the hill a quarter mile from the abandoned parking lot where Zach was meeting me. I spotted him immediately as I pulled in.

He got out of his car and walked over to my passenger door, which I had opened. Not looking at me, he pulled out the box. "Thank you for returning it. I hope you are doing okay."

I nodded. "You know, it won't bother me if you come back to our church."

"I appreciate that, but I'm going somewhere else."

He walked back to his car as if I were a stranger.

I adjusted the rearview mirror, hoping I would see his car circle back around to tell me he was sorry, he'd realized he made a mistake, and that I was the one. But only the reflection of the girl wanting a man to choose her caught my eyes.

I drove away, trying to navigate confusion, loss, pain, and loud silence, feeling like an outsider in my own life. "I go to church, God. I serve. I do all the right things. He was the missing piece, the one to make me complete, and he doesn't want me. What's next? Isn't a husband the ending God's daughters are supposed to get?"

The weeks turned into months, and slowly the ache lessened. I wasn't okay but I knew I would be. I spent more time planning service events for our church and fixing up the house so I could hopefully get approval to buy it. I also spent less time overthinking, less time trying to make the breakup make sense, less time searching for a why or to know which one of us was to blame, and less time worrying if my life looked perfect, analyzing all its flaws, and giving excuses. I spent more time embracing the fact that Daniel would be coming home for the summer after completing his second year of college, that Ember would have only one more year left in middle school, and that we would be taking a week-long scenic road trip to reconnect. I spent less time searching for certainty, less time on the phone with a friend who called to tell me about new forgery charges Gary Richard was facing, and less time caring or searching for more details. I also noticed a shift from my focus on the fantasy of what I didn't get in relationships with men to the reality of what I had, which was life—a good life.

Four months after my breakup with Zach, I stood at the sink with my hands immersed in hot soapy water, doing dishes. Later that day I was set to drive to the title company to sign papers on the house. I watched the sunlight through the mini-blind dance freely within the branches of the trees, mirroring how I felt inside that this day had arrived. I felt proud of myself that the view from the blind at age thirty-seven was so different from what it had been when I was twenty-seven, peering through the blind as a hostage in my home, waiting for Gary Richard to pull from the drive of our old house.

It felt like a lifetime ago, but at the same time, it felt like yesterday. It had been ten years since our divorce—since that moment when I didn't know what life would look like for the kids and me and I worried if I would ever be able to do any of this on my own.

I pulled into the parking lot of the title company, still taking in the surrealness of the moment. For a split second I remembered all those years before when I'd gone to the mortgage company to try to keep our home and had read the words on the door: Closed for lunch.

Not today. Today I was a different woman—with a different experience.

I stepped from my car and walked proudly and confidently inside the building.

The closing manager was standing at the counter waiting for my arrival. She greeted me with a smile. "Caroline?"

I nodded.

"I have everything ready for you in the conference room. Just follow me. It's down the hall."

We sat at the end of a long table that stretched across the center of the room.

"This is your file." She brushed the top of the beige folder with red tabs sticking out the sides. "Your sister and brother-in-law already signed all the seller paperwork this morning." She lifted the top page. "I have all the lines marked where you need to sign, but there are several pages. All in all, I don't think this should take us too long." She handed me a pen. "You ready?"

I smiled as she slid the first paper toward me, feeling my heart bloom like the roses on the bush Daniel and Ember got me for Mother's Day a year after we moved in, nine years before.

She slid paper after paper my way, explaining each one as she gave it to me, but I couldn't hear her because I was lost in the memories of everything it took to get me there. The ink was a thread flowing across time. I was doing so much more than signing papers to take ownership of a house. I was signing for every bill I couldn't pay over the years. I was signing for all the times I worried about putting meals on the table. I was signing for all the times I had hidden from my children behind a locked bathroom door, muffling cries of exhaustion, fear, and hurt, not knowing if we'd be okay. I was signing for the million wrong choices that always seemed to outweigh the thousand right ones. I was signing for all the moments that had led me here.

I left the office and pulled into the grassy parking area in my backyard, gazing at my home with gratitude, thinking how blessed I was. My eyes didn't see the chips on the corners of the walls as damage; they saw the marks made when children had bounced balls, laughed, and played. I didn't see the brown stains on the ceiling as remnants of a leaky roof; I saw the love in the servant hands of my dad and brother-in-law bringing buckets to catch the drips.

My eyes saw a home, our home, filled with precious flaws, authentic scars of beautiful trauma, the divine discoloration of expectant plans, and the gifts of sacrificial love. It was like my soul had landed on contentment's shore, and I was no longer ashamed of my life, my home, or the choices I had made. I saw the happy ending from the beginning.

I also saw that I was complete with or without a man. I saw how my egg donations had put food on my table, and realized that act was about a mother's love and survival—and there was nothing shameful about that. I saw how people who adopted us as a family for Christmas, who placed secret Santa money on my desk, and who bought clothes and shoes for my children represented their servants' hearts and not a dig at my pride. I saw how people freely gave what they could, from furniture to finances to cars to their time to help a single mom rise. I saw how the DNA of my son was the indisputable evidence to hold Gary Richard accountable for his actions and bring justice to all the survivors of his crimes, including me.

I leaned into the pool of sunlight on the windowsill and closed my eyes as a smile splashed across my face and flooded my body with joyful thoughts of being free, a girl, uncoded. *What's next for a woman like me?*

Will I dance in the mysteries of what I have yet to see? Wade gracefully in the unknowns? Wobble beyond the light of my own certainties? Walk alongside my children as they travel through fatherless wounds as adults? Wonder, as time passes, if they feel I did the right things? I didn't know, but as the setting sun began to wash the living room with a golden light, I knew I would never face life alone, because the evidence of God's love and acceptance were blessings woven in the DNA of my soul.

EPILOGUE

When I began to write this book, I set out to tell how my son's DNA was evidence used to convict his father and how my children and I struggled to make it through. But as my fingers stroked the computer keys, much like the sheriff's had nearly twelve years before, a new "start from the beginning" narrative began to show the places in which I still hadn't let go. What was I holding on to? Did I even know?

I knew I never wanted to be a stereotype, another hard-luck story, or a victim, so it was eye-opening when those were the dark portraits exposed. As the words poured forth, I began to see the only one holding my life hostage was me.

Each chapter became a chromosomal strand, an account paired with its lesson. As they took their shape throughout the pages, encoded with their reflections, they mirrored back the girl within me who hadn't found self-acceptance. As patterns repeated throughout the genetic code, it showed the little girl inside needing to be known. With awareness, contentment, and grace, sentence after sentence formed a base, the structure slowly twisted, and the backbone of my story began to appear.

Where I once held on to the drama of adultery and betrayal, I was now blessed to feel free of bitterness. Where I had once seen only chaos and convictions, I now felt the blessings of contentment and redemption. Where I had once felt comparison and shame, I now knew the blessings of acceptance and broken chains. Where struggle and poverty once plagued my days, I now had the blessings of peace and prosperity.

As the veil lifted, the portrayal shifted, and I didn't only see places that felt wrong in my so-called life; I could see all the traces of where it went right and the blueprint behind how each strand was beautifully arranged.

I was a little girl who had gotten lost within the sense of touch; at age twelve, I gave too much. Later I became a teenage mother to a son whose DNA would years later convict his father. In marriage, I thought I had found my purpose, and with divorce, it was lost. The search for stability began in the arms of men, and in the imbalance of it all, they became transactions. Then, through a glass door, I began to see the other side of the frame, and it didn't look quite the same.

Through the sense of touch, the woman inside was found, twelve years after my divorce. And like the woman in the Bible who for twelve years struggled with the issue of blood, then received a healing touch (see Mark 5:25–34), my bleeding stopped as I reached out to another Son born to a teenage mother—Jesus. In His spiritual arms, I found a connection, direction, safety, and trust. By His DNA, like the Israelites who wandered in the desert for nearly forty years (see Deuteronomy 29:3–6), I had been set free because of the relationship He chose to have with me.

For so long, I wanted a different story. I wanted the fairy tale, the happily-ever-after ending, and it turned out I had been living in one since the beginning.

I was no longer locked in the tower of self-contempt, restrained by my mind. I could see my rescuer had been here the whole time. He wasn't lost or in a land far, far away. He was there the whole time. He opened the window of my soul and patiently waited for me to invite Him in and to believe that by the gift He freely gave me, I was already free.

With every strand of identifiable grace interlaced, the ladder of unconditional love unfolded. As I climbed down, there He was kneeling on the ground with His arms reached out. I could feel the warmth of His touch before I fell into His embrace. My face pressed into the firmness of His presence—His goodness and the completeness of His love as He revealed who He was.

My daughter. Billions of years ago, I sculpted a key that was beautiful and unique. I placed it inside your genes, so whenever darkness came to try and shackle your light, you could always turn the key toward My love to set you free.

Remember to look around when uncertainty comes your way, making you question if My presence has dispersed. Watch as the branches of the trees sway on top of a sturdy base, hear the lullaby in the rain, feel as the atmosphere turns into a breath, taste the flavors of the seasons, smell the flowers kissed by the sun. And see within My blessings all things are one.

Majestically I will be your guide as you navigate the unknowns of your life, and as My love forever plays Pachelbel's Canon in D, I will delight as your soul sways free, for you are My masterpiece.

ACKNOWLEDGMENTS

Writing is hard, impostor syndrome is real, and this memoir couldn't have been written without you. You, my sister, who answered my phone calls and patiently listened as I repeated sentences over and over. You, my friends, who responded to all my random texts for opinions and feedback. You, TJ, who gave me so much advice you should have charged. You, my prayer warriors, who never ceased covering me and this book in prayer. You, as in everyone who believed, encouraged, taught, supported, prayed, and spoke life into me and my dream. I thank you!

I'd also like to thank—

You, the reader, for your time, support, and willingness to take this journey. I appreciate you!

My children, for being my why, my reasons, my greatest blessings. You have had front-row seats and behind-the-scenes access to all of this. I have felt your support and seen the sacrifices. I love you and am so proud of who you are.

My parents, for your endless support, love that never ends, and doing all you did to raise us the best you knew how.

Ginger Kolbaba. You took your last breath on earth as we were on the final chapter. There isn't a day that goes by I don't think about you and every breath you contributed to keep this book alive. You took a chance on me, you saw things within me that I didn't, and you helped shape the manuscript in ways I couldn't. This book exists because you did.

Brooke Warner, Shannon Green, Crystal Patriarche, Sheila Trask, Tabitha Bailey, Rylee Warner, and the whole She Writes Press and BookSparks Teams. Thank you for the encouragement, the direction, the handholding, the community, and the countless ways you educate and support your authors. Above all, thank you for being an embodiment of what a publisher should be: transparent, knowledgeable, forward-thinking, unafraid to take risks, and unapologetic for the fact that writing should be based on more than notoriety or the size of an author's platform, that our stories matter, and we absolutely have a right to tell them.

Much love.

ABOUT THE AUTHOR

Brandi Dredge is a mom, encourager, and author. She shares her story with the hopes that what she went through will bring encouragement to victims and/or individuals who could benefit from knowing about God's favor and blessings in their lives. She enjoys swimming in the deep end of mystical thoughts, wading in emotions to pen poetry, and sipping a strong cup of coffee. She is a member of The National Association of Memoir Writers and resides in St. Joseph, Missouri.

Looking for your next great read?

We can help!

Visit www.shewritespress.com/next-read
or scan the QR code below for a list
of our recommended titles.

She Writes Press is an award-winning
independent publishing company founded to
serve women writers everywhere.